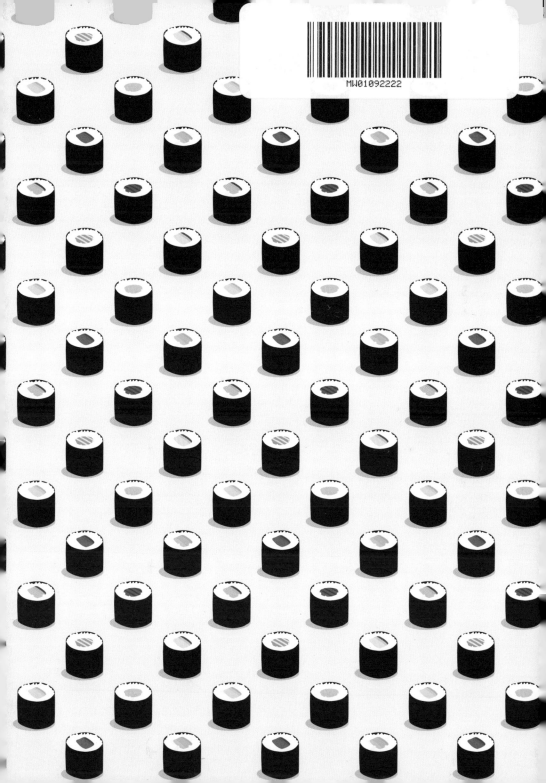

OISHII

OISHII

THE HISTORY OF SUSHI

ERIC C. RATH

REAKTION BOOKS

For my students

Published by
REAKTION BOOKS LTD
Unit 32, Waterside
44–48 Wharf Road
London N1 7UX, UK
www.reaktionbooks.co.uk

First published 2021
Copyright © Eric C. Rath 2021

Printed and bound in India by Replika Press Pvt. Ltd

A catalogue record for this book is available from the
British Library

ISBN 978 1 78914 383 6

CONTENTS

INTRODUCTION: WHAT IS SUSHI?

Sushi, arguably the most minimalistic dish ever created, has also become complicated and diverse. Nothing seems to epitomize simplicity as much as nigirizushi, a single slice of fish over rice. Sushi rolls (makizushi, also known as norimaki) were also once as simple, with only prosaic ingredients such as dried gourd (kanpyō) rolled up with rice into a tube of nori. But today practically anything can be stuffed into a sushi roll or spread on top: fried shrimp, cream cheese or Spam. Sushi rolls can be made 'inside out' with the rice on the exterior. The rolls are also sometimes breaded and fried. They can be topped with slices of fish, prawns, avocado, fried Japanese breadcrumbs or fried onions. Sometimes they are slathered with different colours of sauce. In short, what was once a lean food of green cylindrical geometry has become, in some instances, an amorphous dripping creature with twice the calories, sodium and cholesterol of a McDonald's hamburger.

Such sushi experimentation might seem new, and inauthentic to some self-described sushi purists, but chefs have been tinkering with the recipe for sushi for millennia. The earliest Chinese examples of sushi, which date from the sixth century, flavoured the rice and fish with orange peel and 'wine' made from grains.[1] One eighteenth-century cookbook in Japan suggested using the skin of the poisonous Japanese blowfish (fugu) or paper instead of nori for makizushi – the paper was discarded before eating the roll.[2] Besides the California roll, which is often scorned by sushi purists as 'inauthentic', there are other 'local' sushi in North America such as the San Francisco roll (made with cucumber, salmon, salmon roe and fresh basil), the Las Vegas roll (shrimp, eel and cream cheese), the Texas roll (freshwater eel, avocado and smelt eggs), which is of course fried, and the Philadelphia roll (cream cheese, smoked salmon, cucumber and avocado).[3] Hawaii, Alaska, New York and Canada have their named rolls as well. The New York roll, for instance, contains pastrami.[4] Sushi rolls have also become supersized to birth the 'sushi burrito'. Sushi bagels, sushi burgers and sushi pizza are all foods that substitute sushi rice for bread and reconstruct the rolls into new shapes. Leaving America, one finds Prague sushi, a nigirizushi of tuna marinated in soy sauce and beer and topped with apple slices. Sushi rolls drenched in panko and fried like tempura before being accented with chilli sauce are popular in South America.[5] The Bratislava roll contains bacon, red pepper, chives and the spicy sheep's cheese bryndza.[6] In 2010 I was surprised to find 'Korean Sushi' on the menu of a Tibetan restaurant in Dawu, Qinghai, China, which turned out to be makizushi stuffed with Spam.

Toppings and fillings may change, but rice is common to all the aforementioned sushi; however, there are types of sushi in Japan that do not use rice at all. Several Japanese cookbooks from the early modern period (defined as the Edo or Tokugawa period, 1600–1868) provide recipes for riceless sushi that substitute the lees (okara) left over from making tofu. Once the soybeans have

Tibetan dumplings (*momo*) and 'Korean Sushi' from the Black Tent Restaurant in Dawu, prefectural country seat of Golog.

been heated and pulverized to extract soy milk to make tofu, the leftover soy lees can be chopped, pan-fried, flavoured and mixed with finely diced vegetables, burdock and mushrooms. *Assemblage of Noted Grain Dishes (Meihan burui)*, published in 1802, indicates that the okara should be mashed, stir-fried in oil and flavoured with Japanese pepper (*sanshō*) before being used as a stuffing for fish. The text even goes so far as to suggest that the fish could be grilled if it smells too fishy.[7] As we can see from this recipe, the word 'sushi' did not necessarily designate a food that was eaten cold, or while the fish was still fresh, or that automatically included rice; indeed, in the earliest recipes for sushi, the rice (or other grain) was probably discarded instead of being eaten after its role in fermentation was finished.

TOFU-LEES SUSHI

The Assemblage of Noted Grain Dishes (Meihan burui), published in
1802, contains 33 sushi recipes, including directions for sushi
using the leftovers from tofu making called okara. In making
tofu, soy milk is extracted from the cooked soybeans. The leftover beans can be fried to make okara. Okara is often augmented
with chopped vegetables to make a salad. In the following recipe
okara is used as a substitute for rice. The fish is unspecified but
the recipe indicates it follows in the pattern of earlier recipes in
the text for striped mullet, silver pomfret and chub mackerel,
suggesting that these would be the types of fish used.

The fish is prepared like any other recipe, but in this case okara is
substituted for rice. Remove and discard any extraneous matter
from the okara, pulverize it in a cooking mortar (suribachi), and
pan-fry it in sesame oil. Add in some powdered Japanese pepper
(sanshō) and mix well; then stuff the mix into the abdomen of
fish. Some may find the fish too raw smelling, so it is fine to
grill them, and that will prevent them from smelling fishy.[8]

THE EARLIEST SUSHI

While it is hard to determine a shared characteristic among all of the various types of sushi available today, what designated the first sushi was neither the use of fish nor rice but the taste, and the taste of sushi may be the origin for its Japanese name. Sushi can be written several different ways in Japanese: the phonetic すし and by the two characters 寿司, which when put together might mean 'felicitous rule' but instead are used solely for their sounds. The combination 寿司 (and its variation 寿し) date to the early modern period, a time when the Japanese developed visual and verbal puns into a popular art form.[9] Two earlier ways of writing sushi as 鮨 and 鮓 originated in China. The first character, pronounced as zhi in Chinese, originally referred to a fermented dish made from salt and fish, according to China's oldest dictionary, the third-century BCE *The Literary*

Sign for a sushi restaurant.

Expositor (Erya). China's third oldest dictionary, the third-century CE Explanation of Names (Shiming), defines the second character – pronounced zha in Chinese – as fish preserved in salt with rice. Both dishes were fermented foods using salt and fish, and their similarity eventually led writers to use them interchangeably. Later in the third century CE they were considered synonyms, referring to a fermented rice and fish dish that is the prototype of the modern sushi known today.[10] When these characters arrived in Japan, the Japanese likewise made no distinction between them and pronounced both as 'sushi', according to Japan's earliest Chinese–Japanese dictionary, compiled around the year 900.[11]

But why did the Japanese call it sushi? When the Japanese adopted Chinese characters, they typically retained the original Chinese pronunciation and also applied the characters to an existing Japanese word to create a Japanese reading. According to one hypothesis that dates to at least the end of the seventeenth century, the Japanese word 'sushi' was derived from the word sui, meaning 'sour tasting'.[12] The fact that the earliest recipes for sushi produced sour and pungent-tasting dishes adds credence to the theory that the word 'sushi' designated a sour food. Indeed, one of the ancient Chinese ways of writing sushi (zha), combines the character for fish (魚) with the one for vinegar (乍), suggesting a sour-tasting fish.[13]

Modern sushi also has a very slight sour taste because the rice is flavoured with vinegar. Vinegar became a sushi ingredient in the seventeenth century, around the time that Japanese philologists theorized that the Japanese word 'sushi' took its name from its sour taste. However, the earliest surviving recipes for sushi, such as the ancient Chinese examples mentioned earlier, did not rely on vinegar. The sour taste of the sushi derived from lactic-acid fermentation.

Nigirizushi platter.

Thus two kinds of sushi exist. The first, and earliest, are sushi that are sour owing to lactic-acid fermentation, and the second are sushi that have a slightly sour taste because of the addition of vinegar. These are the two major categories of sushi, and the history of sushi can be told, as it is in this book, as the story of a transition away from the ancient method of lactic-acid fermentation to other techniques, such as using vinegar. Sushi thus evolved from a method to preserve fish (and other animal proteins) using fermentation to a means of simply serving fish with rice with a slight vinegary taste.

Both sushi flavoured with vinegar and sushi using lactic-acid fermentation rely on rice (or another grain), but in different ways. Rice flavoured with vinegar (and usually salt and sugar as well) plays a key role in the taste and mouthfeel of nigirizushi and makizushi. It provides a backdrop for appreciating the fish. Some sushi experts judge the quality of sushi restaurants largely

Crucian carp.

on how well the rice is prepared.[14] In contrast, the taste of the rice in lactic-acid sushi is secondary to its main function as a medium for fermentation. Rice contains starch, which breaks down into glucose. Lactic-acid bacteria feed on the glucose to produce lactic acid, which transforms food. First, it acts as a preservative. Lactic acid lowers the pH of the perishable food and inhibits the growth of microbes that could cause diseases or could otherwise contaminate the end product. Second, lactic acid imparts tartness. Lactic-acid fermentation is the reason why yoghurt has a sour taste.[15] Finally, lactic-acid fermentation breaks down the proteins in animal or fish flesh into amino acids. If the process continues for long enough, it will also render the bones soft enough to eat.[16] In contrast to sushi that rely on vinegar, which are best eaten immediately after they are made, lactic-acid fermentation takes time. Some examples of lactic-acid sushi can take up to two years or more to reach their peak flavour.[17] One of these is *funazushi*, which can be made in a few months, but three- or five-year-old examples are especially prized by funazushi fans.[18]

FUNAZUSHI

Funazushi is the foremost example of a type of Japanese sushi that relies on lactic-acid fermentation. The sushi is made from crucian carp (*funa*) found in freshwater streams and lakes such as Lake Biwa in Shiga Prefecture. The key points of funazushi preparation can be understood from a family recipe from the Sugimoto household from the city of Nagahama in Shiga Prefecture. Although their recipe uses modern materials, the Sugimoto family have worked as fishermen on Lake Biwa for generations.

FUNAZUSHI

5 kg (11 lb) salt-cured *nigorobuna* (shiokiribuna)
6.3 litres (26¼ cups) cooked rice that has been cooled

Wash the fish to remove the salt. Use a wire brush to remove the scales as if you were polishing the fish, then wash the fish well. Drain the fish for several hours to allow them to dry. Line a lidded bucket, such as one used for making pickles, with two plastic bags and then place the rice and fish inside together. Close first one bag, then the other. Wrap plastic twine around the bucket [to give it strength] and put on the floating lid. Place a heavy stone on top of the lid.[19]

Nigorobuna (*Carassius auratus grandoculis*) is the species of crucian carp native to Lake Biwa that is preferred for funazushi. They are about the length of a hand. The recipe specifically calls for *shiokiribuna*, which refers locally to nigorobuna that have been cured in salt. Notes to the recipe suggest that the shiokiribuna can be purchased from a fish seller, but they can also be prepared at home. Shiokiribuna are made by first removing all of the

Keisai Eisen, *Koi*, *c.* 1842, woodblock print.

internal organs of the fish except for the roe. Then the fish are doused with salt and packed in a bucket with more salt for a period of several months. The buckets vary in size: those with a 12 kg (26½ lb) capacity have a 39 cm (15 in.) diameter and are 30 cm (12 in.) high.[20] As in the recipe here, the bucket has a heavy stone placed on top of a floating lid that sits on top of the contents of the bucket instead of resting on the bucket's sides. The purpose of the stone is to seal the container and force the lid down on the contents of the bucket, thereby pressing out any moisture. Any liquid that emerges is discarded, since the purpose of the salt curing is to remove the moisture from the fish. If the fish is salted in April using freshly caught carp, which are laden with eggs in that period, then the fish will be fully cured by mid-July to be made into funazushi.[21] Mid-July to mid-August is thought to be the best time to make funazushi because that is when the weather is warm and the fish is fully cured. The sushi is ready to be eaten three months later if the bucket is placed in a sunny spot.

This recipe is a dry version of typical funazushi. Most recipes call for water to be added to the bucket. The water acts as a barrier to prevent oxygen from interacting with the ferment, which could inhibit anaerobic lactic-acid fermentation. Instead of water, the recipe above uses plastic bags to seal the fermenting materials, and it is supposed to result in a funazushi that does not produce a foul smell while it is fermenting.[22] Funazushi recipes can have many other variations, such as in the amount of salt used, the variety of rice, the degree to which the rice is cooked and the period for which everything is allowed to mature.[23] As noted earlier, the rice is generally not meant to be consumed, and it has the consistency of porridge when the fermentation has run its course. Nevertheless, some people do eat the rice, and some recipes for funazushi replace the rice partway through the fermentation process to make it more palatable.[24] One early nineteenth-century recipe for funazushi suggested that the best way to enjoy the dish was to discard the rice used to prepare the sushi and replace it with freshly cooked rice that had been allowed to cool.[25]

With its use of plastic bags and buckets, the recipe above is a modern adaptation, but one cannot assume that other recipes for funazushi used today are more authentic, notwithstanding claims that funazushi is often said to be the most ancient form of sushi in Japan.[26] Sushi made by lactic-acid fermentation did exist in ancient Japan, and it has even older antecedents in China, but the recipe for funazushi has changed considerably in the last centuries. According to sushi scholar Hibino Terutoshi, the modern recipe for funazushi is only about two hundred years old.[27] Today, it is made in the summertime, and it is allowed to ferment for months, if not years, but a recipe in the anonymous cookbook *Assembly of Standard Cookery Writings* (Gōrui nichiyō ryōrishō), published in 1689, indicates that the dish, named for the province Gōshū (an older name for Shiga Prefecture), was made quite differently.

THE FUNAZUSHI OF GŌSHŪ

Ferment this in midwinter. Take the gills and remove the internal organs from them, and flatten the heads of the fish. Pile a large amount of salt on a tray and press both sides of the fish on the salt. Just coat the fish with salt and it is ready to be made into sushi. Steam glutinous brown rice and allow it to cool, then mix in some salt for flavouring. Pack the fish [in a pickling bucket] with a lot of rice. [Using a heavy stone on the floating lid], make sure to apply considerable pressure at the start, but after twenty days, the weight should be lightened, as in a typical sushi recipe. If everything turns out well after seventy days, the sushi will last indefinitely. By summer or autumn of the next year, the taste will be ideal, and the bones will also be soft. When removing the sushi, take off the weight and pour off the water on top of the lid, then readjust the shape of the rice and the fish inside the barrel before replacing the lid and stone; cover again with water as before.[28]

The recipe in *Assembly of Standard Cookery Writings* indicates that funazushi should be made from fresh fish in the winter as opposed to salt-cured fish in the summer, which is customary today. The use of glutinous brown rice is also remarkable; other sushi recipes in *Assembly of Standard Cookery Writings* call for polished non-glutinous rice.[29] The consensus among scholars is that funazushi today may use lactic-acid fermentation like ancient sushi, but the modern recipe is quite different from the

FUNAZUSHI

Some early modern recipes for sushi use sake, kōji or vinegar to hasten the fermentation process creating a style of sushi called 'fresh matured sushi' (*namanare*) (see Chapter Two). The recipe in *Cooking and Flavouring Collection* (*Ryōri anbaishū*), published in 1668, provides an option of adding either older sake and/or vinegar to funazushi depending on when the cook wanted the sushi to be ready. The old sake is not an aged sake, but rather one that is showing its age but has not completely spoiled yet. The advantage of this namanare method is that it cuts the time needed to make funazushi from months to days and makes the rice more palatable, although the sushi is not fully fermented.

Boil together 1.8 litres [7½ cups] of older sake with 540 millilitres [2¼ cups] of salt. If you desire to eat the sushi within two or three days, add 180 millilitres [¾ cup] of vinegar. If you plan to leave the sushi for five to six days, it is not necessary to add the vinegar. Make the rice as usual but with a little less water. After cooling the rice, mix in the solution of salt and sake. It should be saltier than rice salted for eating. Make sure the crucian carp are dried, then salt them, setting them aside for a while so that the moisture disappears. Wash them briskly not allowing them to soak. Combine the ingredients packing the fish with the rice. Use the appropriate amount of rice for the carp. If the plan is to let this rest for five or six days [in a pickling bucket], make the rice saltier. When pressing the sushi in a bucket, for the first two hours, use a lighter weight, and gradually increase the heaviness. The lid can be removed [and the sushi served] after about ten days in the winter, but if one desires to make a less fermented sushi, then five to six days in winter will suffice. Wait longer for larger carp.[30]

Funazushi.

dish created in the ancient, medieval or early modern periods.[31] Comparing recipes from different historical periods can show that sushi, even supposedly the most 'ancient' examples, is not a food that is frozen in time, but instead demonstrates a development that can be traced in the historical record.

When funazushi is served today, the fish is sliced crosswise into thin slivers that are laid across the rice to reconstitute the shape of the fish, with the tail at one end and the head at the other. Female funa are generally prized over males because they retain their orange roe that fill the fish's cavity. Fermentation reduces the flesh of the fish down to a layer a few millimetres in thickness. Without the roe, the flesh of the funa is about the thickness of a slice of ham or salami.

Funazushi gives off the odour of blue cheese, but the initial taste and mouthfeel of the fish is like prosciutto or salami, depending on the thickness of the slice. The taste of cured meat quickly gives way to a punch of sourness that originates at the back of the mouth and often causes a physical reaction. When

I eat funazushi, I cannot help but pucker my lips and turn my head to confront the sour assault on my mouth. The rice is the sourest part of the funazushi and has a texture reminiscent of cold millet that has been boiled to the point that it has lost its granularity. No semblance of rice in terms of shape or taste remains, which is why most people do not eat it. Funazushi alone would not make a satisfying meal. Indeed, trying to finish a whole fish oneself is a challenge, although fans of funazushi will even swish the head in hot tea before swallowing it. Funazushi is the sourest thing I have ever tasted and the tartness stayed in my mouth the next day like bile after a hangover.

Were lactic-acid sushi the only form of sushi today, the dish would be no more than a culinary oddity, instead of a poster child for Japan's national food culture. A 2015 Internet survey in Japan of 1,000 people aged between 20 and 59 found that almost 85 per cent of men and 89 per cent of women liked sushi, but only 5.9 per cent had ever tried funazushi. The most popular types of sushi that respondents ate instead were versions sold at convenience stores and supermarkets – some 43.3

Nigirizushi and makizushi.

per cent indicated that they purchased sushi from such locations monthly.[32] These popular varieties are, of course, the types of sushi recognized globally as 'sushi' today, namely, nigirizushi and makizushi.[33] In 1968, when food critic Craig Claiborne declared that sushi was Japan's 'national dish', he was referring to nigirizushi, 'an assortment of small morsels of the freshest raw fish and sea food pressed onto cold rice lightly seasoned with vinegar'.[34] Fifty years later, nigirizushi and makizushi remain synonymous with sushi both inside and outside of Japan. However, these are only two varieties of sushi, and both are relatively recent innovations compared to the long history of sushi made with lactic-acid fermentation in China and Japan.

CHALLENGES IN TRACING THE HISTORY OF SUSHI

Tracing the history of sushi poses challenges, and both popular and academic accounts of it in English contain errors. There is even a lack of consensus about events that happened in the United States little more than fifty years ago, such as when the first California roll was invented and when the first Los Angeles restaurant installed a case at their sushi counter in which to display ingredients. The most often cited English-language books about sushi are by Sasha Issenberg, Theodore Bestor and Trevor Corson. Reporter Sasha Issenberg celebrates how sushi has gone global in terms of its sourcing and popularity, and traces how a bluefin tuna from the Atlantic can wind up in the Tsukiji fish market in Tokyo.[35] Anthropologist Theodore Bestor has offered a vibrant profile of Tsukiji, which from 1923 until its move in 2018 served as the economic hub of the fish and food trade in Japan and was a popular site for tourists seeking to peruse the stalls and watch the bluefin tuna auctions.[36] Trevor Corson colourfully recounts the course of study at a school for sushi-making in California.[37] Cognizant of the continued salience of these works, in writing this book, I offer corrections where needed but have focused on aspects of the history of sushi that have yet to be told.

Recipes do not reveal the whole story of sushi, and the words for different types of sushi in Japan appeared centuries before the first recorded recipes, so we cannot be sure exactly how the most ancient forms of sushi were made. Cookbooks began including recipes for sushi in the early modern period, but we cannot assume that these recipes record the exact methods used in that era (or earlier) to make sushi. Recipes are prescriptive of the ways foods should be, not an accurate document of how people actually cooked and ate. Early modern Japanese cookbooks in particular were made for a male reader-ship that included professional chefs, as well as amateur cooks and readers who simply enjoyed exploring cooking vicariously. Early modern cookbook writing was often similar to a genre of fiction, including recipes and entire menus that few, if any, readers could create in real life.[38] Most early modern cookbooks focused on food for special occasions. Only a very few of them provided instructions to novice chefs on how to cook rice or prepare typical daily foods such as pickles. Similar to pickles, sushi began as a preserved food, and might appear as a side dish at a banquet in premodern Japan, but not as a main course. Sushi was too prosaic, and before the nineteenth century, it was not considered a great delicacy. The nigirizushi that is considered to be the representative form of sushi today and a symbol of Japanese culinary culture did not even warrant mention in recipe collections of the early modern period because it was considered street food, an inexpensive snack to be eaten casually.[39]

WHAT, THEN, IS SUSHI?

Despite occasional claims that different forms of sushi were invented by someone or other, sushi is not the creation of a single person; it instead represents the world's most prominent anonymous cuisine. Sushi is not a cuisine in the sense of a national, regional or local way of cooking. Sushi is a cuisine because it provides a variety of ways of working with and thinking about ingredients that transcend national boundaries. Sushi may be associated with Japan – and Japanese governmental and non-governmental agencies have worked and continue to work to try to brand sushi as 'Japanese' – but sushi was never solely a Japanese dish. Today, anyone can make their own sushi roll and put anything they want in it, and even deep-fry it, should they choose to.

Sushi was not invented in Japan, but anonymous Japanese chefs helped to create many new versions of sushi that are profiled in this book, which aims to clarify sushi's long and diverse history. It may be a representative Japanese food, but it was not found throughout all of Japan historically. There is no evidence that the Ainu living in Hokkaido made sushi before the Meiji period (1868–1912), nor is sushi part of Okinawa's traditional food culture until the modern age.[40] Sushi is a very simple food, but it is often exoticized, which is another reason why we need a careful exposition of where sushi came from, how it developed and how it might change in the future.

The Japanese developed numerous forms of sushi over the course of more than a millennium, and sushi has become synonymous with Japanese cuisine, so it makes sense to trace the history of sushi through reference to Japan. The challenge to this is the fact that the first complete Japanese recipes for sushi date to some eight hundred years after the word sushi was first used in that country.

Uogashi standing sushi bar, Shibuya, Tokyo, 2017.

The earliest sushi recipes relied on freshwater fish such as carp, but today a bewildering array of fish and seafood can be found at sushi restaurants. Sushi chef Meguro Hidenobu in an encyclopaedia of sushi techniques lists 45 varieties of fish and 29 types of seafood toppings called *tane* for nigirizushi.[41] Sushi scholar Ōkawa Tomohiko tabulated a similar list of 86 marine ingredients.[42] Part of the enjoyment of eating sushi is this choice of fish and seafood, whether one orders oneself or relies on the chef to suggest combinations. Price, location and seasonality will determine what one eats, but a typical nigirizushi selection might include shrimp, octopus, omelette, squid, salmon, tuna, eel, halibut and other choices. A set nigirizushi dinner or lunch will usually include a sushi roll. Pickled and fresh vegetables, egg and other ingredients can be combined into various makizushi, as noted earlier. Sushi restaurants also serve sliced fish called sashimi. Today, both sushi and sashimi are eaten with a little soy sauce, an accompaniment popularized in the 1800s when soy sauce became more prominent as a condiment. Some sushi restaurants provide customers with large amounts of spicy green wasabi. Most wasabi today is a paste made from less expensive

Wasabi and specialized wasabi grater made of wood and angel shark skin.

horseradish or from the leafy 'field wasabi' (*hatake wasabi*) plant, rather than the costly wasabi root ground in more upscale sushi establishments. There, the chefs might restrict the wasabi they serve to a slight amount added directly to certain sushi. The custom of filling the dish used for soy sauce with a mound of wasabi before mixing it into a slurry in which to dunk and saturate the sushi is anathema because it destroys the subtle taste of the fish and dilutes the wasabi. Pickled ginger (*shōga* or *gari*) is another favourite accompaniment to sushi. Eating a slice of ginger pickled in the brine of salted apricots (*ume*) is a refreshing way to cleanse the palate between one delicate piece of sushi and another. Both wasabi and ginger are said to have antibacterial properties that prevent food poisoning.[43]

Nigirizushi and makizushi have entered into the global culinary lexicon, so they will not appear in italics in this book.

Other Japanese terms will be in italics when they first appear and the most important of these terms related to sushi can be found in the Glossary. Like all Japanese words, sushi can be singular or plural. In Japanese compounds, the 's' in sushi becomes a 'z' – thus makizushi, not makisushi (although English renderings of maki sushi and nigiri sushi sometimes appear).

This book includes recipes that help document the historical development and variety of sushi. Premodern recipes often omit crucial steps either because the chef was assumed to know what to do or because the dishes were meant as a form of literature to be read and not actually prepared. In any case, these recipes show the many ways that food writers imagined sushi through the centuries. Those recipes that do include measurements (and many do not) favour measurements by volume instead of weight in traditional increments of shō (1.8 litres,

Scallop nigirizushi.

1.9 quarts) or *gō* (180 ml, 6 oz). The distinct sake bottles sold in Japan have a capacity of one *shō*, an amount that is ten individual servings of one *gō* each. I have translated these traditional measurements into litres and U.S. legal cup size, which is 8 U.S. fluid ounces. I have not had the gumption or materials to test the historical recipes, but the ones I created for chirashizushi, persimmon leaf sushi and sanmazushi work even in rural Kansas and are usually delicious (*oishii*).

As a historian of Japanese dietary culture and someone who is old enough to have witnessed the 1980s sushi boom and the subsequent transformation of sushi from an elite food to one that is now ubiquitous, I marvel at the ways sushi has evolved. Sushi's history is fascinating in its own right, but its story can also tell us how one food has changed to meet the needs and desires of an increasing number of consumers as it has matured into a global cuisine. Few other foods are as versatile, long-lived or varied as sushi.

ONE
SEARCHING FOR THE ORIGINS OF SUSHI

Lacking physical remains, sushi, like many foodstuffs, has not survived in the archaeological record, which means that the earliest history of sushi must be traced through written accounts, the oldest of which comes from China. Unfortunately, the earliest Chinese recipes for sushi appear several hundred years after the Chinese words for sushi first debuted, raising questions about what the first sushi actually was. In Japan, too, the earliest references to sushi provide little, if any, indication of how sushi was made. To fill in these gaps, Japanese historians of sushi have focused on tracing how the key ingredients for sushi came together, logically hypothesizing that the first people who fermented fish with grain and salt must have had these ingredients close at hand. Given that sushi today is made almost exclusively with polished rice, and rice has long been associated with Japanese civilization, Japanese scholars have focused on places where rice agriculture occurred either in paddy or on dry fields as the birthplace of sushi, and that led them to Southeast Asia. Making sushi synonymous with rice has also allowed Japanese scholars to explain why and when sushi arrived in

Japan, by assuming that sushi came with rice paddy agriculture, which they have seen as central both to the Japanese diet and to Japanese society. However, recent archaeological evidence and historical research have not only changed the chronology of rice's arrival in Japan, they have also clarified that rice was never the main staple grain for Japan's population until several thousand years after it began being cultivated in Japan. Thus, although rice had considerable symbolic importance, and it was used as a currency for paying taxes to the central government, it was not Japan's main food source for most of its population until the early modern period (1600–1868) at the earliest. In this light, a review of the earliest records of sushi in China and Japan should force us to question the assumption that sushi is necessarily a rice-based food, particularly since rice may have served only as a medium for lactic-acid fermentation (and need not have been consumed). Expanding the definition of sushi to include foods made with grains other than rice not only raises the possibility that sushi was more widely consumed in ancient Japan when rice formed only a small portion of most people's diets, but prioritizes the process of how sushi was made as a manner of defining it, as opposed to limiting 'sushi' to foods only made with certain ingredients. This chapter reviews the evidence to determine what we can know about the earliest sushi on record.

THE FIRST HISTORICAL REFERENCES IN CHINESE SOURCES

Sushi began as a fermented food. Fermented and pickled meat and fish are mentioned in Chinese Zhou dynasty (c. 1046–256 BCE) sources, but these foods were not widely consumed until the early Han dynasty (206 BCE–220 CE).[1] The Chinese characters zhi and zha that now mean sushi originally designated different

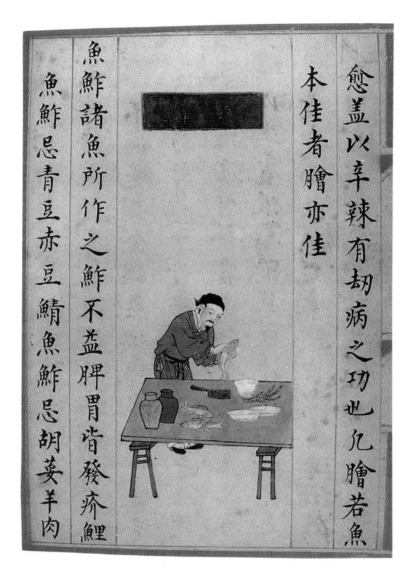

愈盖以辛辣有劫病之功也凡膾若魚

本佳者膾亦佳

魚鮓諸魚所作之鮓不益脾胃皆發疥癩

魚鮓忌青豆赤豆鯖魚鮓忌胡荽羊肉

Illustration of salted fish (*yuzha*) from *Materia dietetica* (*Shiwu bencao*), a dietetic herbal in four volumes dating from the Ming dynasty.

PICKLED FISH (*ZHA*)

This recipe is from the earliest Chinese agricultural manual, *The Important Arts for the People's Welfare* (Qimin yaoshu), compiled in the mid-sixth century, and provides the oldest directions for making sushi. Besides being the oldest recipe, the directions are by far the most detailed in any premodern source on how to make sushi by lactic-acid fermentation.

Take a fresh carp, the larger the better . . . After the scales are removed, the fish is cut into pieces about five inches long, one inch wide and half an inch thick. As a piece is cut, it is placed into a basin of water. Clean off the blood as the piece is soaked. When all the pieces are sliced and washed, strain off the water, return to a basin of fresh water, wash and strain again. The pieces are placed on a plate, mixed evenly with white salt and transferred onto a basket. The basket is placed on a horizontal stone tablet to allow the water in the fish to drain away. We call the salt, 'chasing water salt', since it expels water as it is absorbed by the fish. If the water in the fish is not thoroughly drained out, the shelf life of the *cha* [zha] will be poor. It is quite safe to allow the water to drain overnight. When the draining of water is complete, roast a piece to check the saltiness of the fish. If it is not salty enough, put more salt in the *sang* [starch substrate in the form of *fan*, cooked rice]. If it is too salty, no salt need be added. After the starch substrate is properly applied, place a layer of salt over the incubating medium.

The starch substrate is prepared by cooking non-glutinous rice. The cooked rice should be on the hard side. It should not be too soft. If it is too soft the fish preserve will spoil more easily. Mix into the rice whole dogwood seeds, finely sliced orange peel, and a little good wine. The function of the spices is to enhance the aroma of the product; thus, only a small amount is needed. If orange peel is not available, one may replace it with *tshao chü tzu* (grass tangerine seeds).[2] Wine [that is, sake] is useful to deter contamination. It will improve the quality of the *cha* [*zha*] and hasten its ripening. Usually for every *tou* [10 litres, 42 cups] of fish pieces, use half a *shêng* [1 litre, 4⅓ cups] of wine.

Layer the fish pieces in a jar. One row of fish is placed beside one row of starch substrate, and repeat until the jar is full ... Finally, cut off strips of bamboo and criss-cross them to form a cover over the mouth of the jar. If bamboo is not available, use strips of bramble. Leave the jar inside the house. Do not expose it to the sun or leave it near the fireplace. Doing so will promote spoilage, and ruin the flavour. In cold weather wrap it liberally with straw. Do not allow it to freeze. When a red liquid oozes over the mat, discard it. When a light liquid comes up and tastes sour, the product is ready. When serving it, tear the pieces by hand. Cutting it with a knife would give it a fishy taste.[3]

foods. The oldest Chinese dictionary, the *Literary Expositor* (*Erya*), dating to the third century BCE, designates the word zhi as fish preserved in salt. The third oldest dictionary, *Explanation of Names* (*Shiming*), completed around 200 CE, referred to zha as a 'pickled food fermented in salt and rice'. For its inclusion of rice, zha is a closer approximation of sushi than zhi. Nevertheless, another dictionary, *The Expanded Literary Expositor* (*Guangya*), compiled around the year 230, pronounced in its commentary on the *Erya* that the two terms were synonymous and that both meant fish pickled in rice.[4] Since that point in the third century, both characters have been used to refer to sushi in China and Japan, albeit that sushi was not always made with rice – or fish.

The recipe for sushi in *The Important Arts for the People's Welfare* directs readers to clean and fillet fresh carp, then salt them to expel moisture from the fish as a means of preserving it. The salted fish, once dried, is added to cooked rice that is also salted. At this point the recipe departs from recipes for lactic-acid sushi found in Japan because it instructs readers to add seasonings, specifically dogwood seeds, orange peel and something called 'grass tangerine seeds'. The same text notes that dogwood can be used with spring onions (scallions) and ginger as a flavouring for tea.[5] Dogwood could refer to the tree *Cornus kousa*, which has edible red berries said to have a bitter taste reminiscent of mango, but with seeds that are too hard to consume.[6] Another possibility is that the dogwood (zhuyu) is actually *shizhuyu* (*Zanthoxylum ailanthoides*), a type of prickly ash that has a taste similar to Japanese pepper (sanshō).[7] These ingredients suggest that the sushi would have had either fruity or slightly spicy notes to accent its overall sour flavour profile derived from the lactic-acid fermentation.

Besides spices, the recipe in *The Important Arts for the People's Welfare* also calls for adding wine for preservation, to improve the taste and facilitate fermentation. This 'wine' is actually a millet or rice beverage similar to a Japanese sake or a beer rather than a grape wine. The same text provides directions for making 38 different alcoholic 'wines' derived from rice and millet.[8] Use of sake or the leftover rice from sake making, both of which can facilitate sushi-making, became more widely added to sushi in early modern Japan, but the Japanese had enjoyed fermented beverages since prehistoric times, so it is possible they could have experimented with adding these to sushi like the Chinese.

One of the distinct features of these early Chinese sushi recipes is that the sushi served as an ingredient for simmered dishes. *The Important Arts for the People's Welfare* contains four recipes for pickled fish added to simmered foods, and one of these is a chowder that derives its name from a Han dynasty story about a chef who made a soup from meat and fish collected from five relatives of the ruler.

FIVE LORDS' SOUP

Finely dice pickled fish and meat on a cutting board. Add water and boil. Use this as the basis for a soup stock.[9]

In China, sushi continued to be enjoyed as a relatively popular dish until the eighteenth century, when taste preferences and methods of food preservation changed. Thereafter, pickled fish recipes survived only as a local food, particularly in southwestern China.[10] The first reference to sushi in Korea dates to 1500.[11]

While the aforementioned sushi recipe calls specifically for using non-glutinous rice, other sushi recipes in *The Important Arts for the People's Welfare* are more ambiguous about the grains to be used. Of the eight recipes, five of them specify rice, although the degree to which that rice is milled is often unclear. The rice would have been much browner than table rice familiar to diners today. One recipe calls for (漬米) (zimi), which is probably rice soaked in water.[12] The other two recipes require steamed millet *fan* (飯) and *baifan* (白飯). The latter is not necessarily white rice and could designate rice grown on a dry field, or it could suggest using a grain such as millet without other cereals mixed with it. Millet was the staple grain for northern China, the area where the author of *The Important Arts for the People's Welfare* lived.[13] The recipe for millet sushi is as follows:

Bucket for making sushi, Gifu Prefecture.

METHOD FOR MAKING PICKLED FISH

After the fish is cut up into pieces, salt it; and after setting it aside for the length of a meal, remove any water that has excreted. Wash the fish well, and pack it with the steamed millet. Do not use salt.[14]

Millet sushi might seem to be an anathema to some sushi purists, but in lactic-acid sushi-making, the purpose of any grain is to provide fuel for fermentation. Cooked millet contains approximately the same amount of carbohydrates as cooked brown rice, meaning that both would be equally as efficacious for lactic-acid sushi. Japanese historians of sushi tend to ignore the possibility that the recipes in The Important Arts for the People's Welfare could be made without rice, because rice agriculture is critical to their theories about the origins of sushi and how sushi came to Japan.

RICE AGRICULTURE AND THE PRESUMED ORIGINS OF SUSHI

Despite the fact that the earliest references to sushi are from China, Japanese sushi historians look to Southeast Asia as the birthplace of sushi. Shinoda Osamu, author of *The Book of Sushi* (*Sushi no hon*), noted the absence of sushi in ancient China and surmised that it was imported from Southeast Asia sometime before the second century.[15] Shinoda pointed to tribes living in the hills of Southeast Asia as the 'inventors' of sushi, but the eminent food scholar Ishige Naomichi instead identified communities practising rice paddy agriculture in northeast Thailand and Laos as sushi's progenitors. Ishige drew these conclusions based on his ethnographic research in these areas and his supposition that sushi originated in a place where the local population had access both to fish and to rice, two ingredients he viewed as indispensable to sushi. In fact, the first fish used for sushi were ones reared in rice paddies, according to Ishige.[16] Both Shinoda and Ishige agree that sushi came to Japan along with rice paddy agriculture around the year 300 BCE, the once widely accepted starting point of the Yayoi period (300 BCE–300 CE).[17] Ishige has long affirmed the centrality of rice to Japanese civilization, so the supposition that sushi arrived with rice not only defines sushi as a 'rice food', it also gives sushi a central place within Japanese (culinary) identity.[18] Despite the fact that these scholars acknowledge the existence of sushi made with other ingredients besides rice, such as foxtail millet (*awa*) or taro (*satoimo*), these forms of sushi do not figure largely in their considerations of the history of sushi. Doing so would not only change their definition of sushi, it would undermine their explanation of how sushi came to Japan.[19]

After Shinoda and Ishige conducted their research, new archaeological findings have pushed the timeline for the arrival of rice to Japan back from around 300 BCE to the first or second millennia BCE. Moreover, an even more important conclusion embraced by many historians is that up to the seventeenth century, rice remained a negligible part of most people's diets in Japan, supplying only around 25 per cent of food energy.[20] Rural populations grew rice in premodern Japan, but they needed it to pay taxes. Tax records, which are abundant, focus on rice paddy agriculture, but tend to ignore other foodstuffs that were not taxed but were more important to the diet of the non-elite. Having paid their taxes in rice, rural populations relied on foraging and planting non-rice grains on mountainsides farmed by slash-and-burn agriculture. Three-quarters of Japan is too mountainous for paddy agriculture, but swidden crops, like buckwheat and varieties of millet, can thrive on slopes up to 30 degrees.[21] As described in more detail below, when ancient Japanese sources mention sushi, it is usually in the context of it being used as a tribute payment, in the same way the central government assessed a tax paid in kind in rice. Consequently, sushi made with rice in the ancient period would have been a prestige food meant for the consumption of the elite.

However, we should not discount the possibility that sushi was made from other grains besides rice and that would have made sushi easier to make and more widely consumed. Millets antedate the arrival of rice to Japan and date to the Neolithic period (10,000–2000/1000 BCE).[22] Although ancient sources are not clear on all the ingredients that could have been used to make sushi, there are examples of sushi from the early modern period made with foxtail millet in the mountainous areas of Gifu, Tokushima and Kōchi Prefectures.[23] Ethnographic surveys about food habits in the 1920s and '30s yielded several varieties of sushi made from grains other than rice. The town of Shichinohe in Aomori was noted for sushi made with foxtail millet. In Wakayama Prefecture several recipes for local sushi used wheat along with rice. In Tokushima barnyard millet (hie) was mixed with rice, but in locales in Shiga Prefecture barley augmented the rice.[24] While we cannot verify whether these 'traditional' forms of non-rice sushi existed in the ancient period, the fact that they survived in the repertoire of Japanese foodways up through the first decades of the twentieth century suggests that it is incorrect to view sushi purely as a 'rice food', especially since the rice in lactic-acid fermented sushi is not usually consumed. Moreover, acknowledging non-rice sushi also opens up new possibilities for considering when and how sushi came to Japan.

RICE-LESS SUSHI

Despite the fact that modern scholars associate sushi with rice, that connection was not the case in the early modern period. There was at least one sushi origin story that circulated in Japan that suggested that sushi did not require any grain at all, and that humans were not the ones to invent it. The culinary text *Assemblage of Noted Grain Dishes* (*Meihan burui*), published in 1802, describes osprey sushi, a kind of sushi made by seabirds who rely on the most basic ingredients to preserve their fish.

> Osprey sushi is a famous product of Kishiwada in Izumi province [modern Osaka Prefecture] and some say it is also used as a tribute gift. It is not made by humans. When a bird called an osprey runs out of things to eat in the middle of winter, it will catch various fish and store them around the water's edge, in sand, and between rocks. The osprey urinates on the fish to prevent other birds from eating them, and the fish becomes fermented with salt water and exposure to the

Osprey preparing to dive at the Kennedy Space Center, Florida, 2004.

rain and the elements. It is uncertain if this story is a fact. It is said that the fish used is an immature mullet.[25]

Sugino Gonuemon, the author of *Assemblage of Noted Grain Dishes*, was a physician from Kyoto, but his book is hardly a medical treatise. Instead, the work is a collection of various methods to prepare grain dishes, recipes that add vegetables, beans or fish to cooked rice and porridges.[26] Scholars include *Meihan burui* among the so-called 'hundred tricks' (*hyakuchin*) cookbooks that showed early modern readers how to prepare a single ingredient – tofu, sea bream or sweet potatoes – dozens of different ways.

The story of osprey sushi appears at the end of *Assemblage of Noted Grain Dishes*, which contains 33 recipes for making sushi, the largest collection among premodern culinary texts. The sushi recipes appear at the end of the cookbook, and it appears that the author has included them with some reluctance, noting in a few lines that sushi is more of a street food than one made at home:

> Sushi became widely known thanks to fishmongers in town and people who were knowledgeable about how to make sushi opening shops. Thus, there is no reason for writing about sushi here, except that by listing the names of sushi and noting their methods of preparations that will provide some guidance for anyone who might otherwise remain completely ignorant about them.[27]

Sugino's recipes are at times terse, which is typical of early modern culinary texts written by and for a male readership who already knew how to cook because they did so professionally or were armchair gourmets who delegated cooking to their household staff. In the age that Sugino was writing, sushi was assuming its modern form and sushi restaurants and food stalls operated in Japan's largest cities, but his last recipe, an entry that really is not a recipe at all, is for the aforementioned osprey sushi.

A remarkable feature of this 'recipe' is that Sugino mentions the taste, something all too many early modern culinary books fail to do for any of the foods they describe how to prepare. Sugino recalled eating osprey sushi:

> I tried some that I received from a friend from Izumi. It was not especially tasty but there was something distinct about it, and I thought it had a certain flavour. However, it is hard to obtain a lot of it because it is given away to connoisseurs or shared among friends. I was unable to eat much of it, so I have now forgotten how it tasted.[28]

Fermented shark (*hákarl*) produced at the Bjarnarhöfn Shark Museum, Iceland, 2015.

Sugino found the taste unique but not memorable. The story of osprey sushi is also mentioned in the *Amusing Laughs* (Kiyū shōran) published in 1830 by Kitamura Nobuyo (1783–1856), who adds that 'the taste is similar to sushi made by people'.[29] Neither author compares the fish to the taste of urine, nor do they recognize the contradiction in the fact that what humans consider a delicacy, the birds who make it will refuse to eat unless they have created it themselves.[30] Osprey sushi is less an origin story or even an accurate depiction of bird life than an interesting tall tale about how one sushi made without grain originated.

While one might dismiss osprey sushi as an odd story, there are fish dishes that self-ferment without rice and give off a strong amino acid, that is, urine, smell, which could suggest that such a form of sushi also existed in Japan. *Hongeo-hoe*, a dish from Jeolla Province in the southwest part of Korea, is made from skate, which as it decays emits uric acid, preserving the fish while at the same time giving a strong smell of urine. When cleaned and then stored in straw, the skate will naturally ferment in twenty to thirty days.[31] Hongeo-hoe is usually served sliced as sashimi with side dishes of pork and kimchi. Another form of self-fermented fish much further from Japan is *hákarl*, fermented shark made in Iceland by cutting the shark into pieces and burying it in gravel pits near the edge of the sea. The seawater washes over the buried shark, which is poisonous to eat raw, and transforms it into a soft preserved food with a strong ammonia odour.[32] The story of osprey sushi involving an unnamed fermented fish that smells like urine may have been invented to explain the particular aroma of preserved skate, a 'sushi' that no longer exists in Japan.

SUSHI IN ANCIENT JAPAN

The question of when sushi arrived in Japan may remain a mystery, but sushi first appears in the historical record in the eighth century CE in several sources where it is mentioned as an item paid in tribute to the imperial court. The *Yōrō Code*, a compilation of laws dating to 718 CE, is the earliest of these references, and it refers to sushi made from mussels, abalone and a 'mixed' sushi, possibly made from those two ingredients or others. A document in the collection of Tōdaiji Temple dated to 737 CE records a payment of a 'mixed sushi' to construction workers and lumberjacks. Archaeologists have also recovered wooden tags used to label goods for transport called *mokkan*, which date to the eighth century CE, that show a wide variety of sushi sent in transport including sea bream, mussel, sweet-fish (*ayu*), sardine, horse mackerel, chub mackerel, salmon and abalone.[33] These eighth-century sources indicate that sushi was differentiated by the type of fish or seafood used as opposed to the grain used to make it; and, during that era, that sushi was considered to be enough of a luxury item that it could be used as a tribute offering to the imperial court or to pay skilled artisans.

The source that provides the clearest information of the use of sushi in paying tribute is the *Procedures of the Engi Era* (*Engi shiki*), a collection of laws and customs completed in 927 that offers insight into how the imperial government was supposed to function. The *Engi shiki* mentions different types of sushi and

'Abalone Sushi', fragment of a wooden tag (*mokkan*, 56 x 22 mm), 8th century, excavated in Nara.

which provinces produced them. Coastal regions such as Wakasa (modern Fukui Prefecture) and Mikawa (Aichi Prefecture) sent sushi made from shellfish such as abalone, sea squirt and mussels. Localities further inland or noted for their rivers such as Mino (southern Gifu Prefecture), Higo (Kumamoto) and Chikuzen (Fukuoka) offered freshwater fish such as sweetfish and crucian carp. The mountainous areas of Iga (Mie), Kii (Wakayama) and Buzen (Fukuoka) sent sushi made from wild boar and venison.[34] Some of these locations in Kyushu were about three weeks away from the court in Kyoto, but others were only a day or two, indicating that the reason for making sushi was not simply to preserve food, but to create a luxury good.[35]

Information revealing how this ancient sushi was made can be gleaned from the *Engi shiki*, although many questions remain. The *Engi shiki* lists a wide variety of sushi: 'mixed sushi' as well as sushi made from abalone, sweetfish, crucian carp, mussel, deer, boar, salmon, sea squirt, large sardines and sea squirt mixed with mussel. Sushi historians surmise that all these ancient forms of sushi used lactic-acid fermentation based upon a reference to a list of ingredients in the *Engi shiki* for sushi made from one part polished rice and 1.3 parts salt to produce ten parts of 'mixed fish sushi'.[36] Most sushi scholars fill in the gaps in the Japanese record by citing the Chinese recipe for pickled fish from *The Important Arts for the People's Welfare*. However, Japanese references to sushi pre-date confirmed references to that text in Japanese libraries by three centuries, and having access to that text is not the same thing as employing the knowledge within it. Administrative and legal texts on agriculture in Japan make no mention of any Chinese agricultural writings due to the geographic and cultural differences between the two countries.[37] So, the methods used in *The Important Arts for the People's Welfare* may not have been applied in Japan.

Maruyama Ōkyo, *Sweetfish in Autumn*, 1785, hanging scroll.

Sea squirts (*hoya*) at Tsukiji Market, Tokyo.

The *Engi shiki* also mentions 'sweet sushi' (*amazushi*), which has given rise to the supposition that that sushi recipe might include kōji, grain inoculated with a mould to facilitate the conversion of starch to sugar and thereby promote fermentation. Kōji is a necessary ingredient to make sake. By the definition of a late seventeenth-century pharmacology text, the *Mirror to Foodstuffs* (Honchō *shokkan*), published in 1697, a 'sweet sushi' was one that used kōji.[38] Sake made with kōji is mentioned in the eighth-century *Geography and Culture of Harima Province* (*Harima fudoki*).[39] However, the first documented use of kōji in sushi-making is from the early modern period.

Various questions remain about how sushi was made and how widely it was consumed in ancient Japan. The twelfth-century collection of Buddhist didactic stories *The Tales of Times*

Funazushi sellers, Omihachiman Shiga Prefecture, 2019.

Now Past (*Konjaku monogatarishū*) suggests that, besides being a tribute item, sushi was a commodity sold by peddlers in the capital. However, 'The Story of the Person Who Saw a Drunken Peddler Woman' raises a clear warning against buying sushi from suspicious people.

According to the story, a man dismounts from his horse near his friend's house and spies a female peddler passed out drunk in a doorway across the lane next to a barrel that contains her wares. He sees her again when he leaves his friend's home and witnesses her vomit into the barrel, catching a glimpse of the sweetfish sushi inside. Caught in the act of vomiting on her sushi, the woman quickly reaches into the bucket and stirs the vomit in with the sushi. Sickened by the scene, the man hurries away. At this point the narrator interjects:

When you think about it, sweetfish sushi is very similar in appearance to vomit, so some unknowing person would not discover what the woman who sold that sushi had done and would have most certainly have eaten it. That is why the man who witnessed this scene refused to eat sweetfish sushi thereafter. Not only did he not eat sweetfish sushi that was sold, he would not even eat sushi prepared in his own home. When someone who hears about all this tells another person, they will say 'don't eat sweetfish sushi,' and prevent them from doing so. And when that person sees sweetfish sushi someplace they are eating, they will probably have a fit and gag before getting up and running out.

In summary, anything sold in the market or by a peddler woman is most certainly contaminated. As this story has shown, even someone wealthy ought to eat only things that were prepared before their very eyes.[40]

Tales of Times Now Past may not condemn all sushi, but it does indicate that the sour smell and taste are reminiscent of vomit to the point that the sushi itself could be vomit. Assuming that the sweetfish sushi was lactic-acid sushi, the rice would have been porridge-like, similar in consistency and smell to vomit. Lactic-acid sushi also has a sour taste similar to bile, something familiar to anyone who has barfed up the contents of their stomach from a hangover. All of these associations provide reasons for people to make their own sushi at home, and the tale suggests that wise people already did that. The commodification of sushi, or other products, is what the tale ultimately warns against, but at the same time documents.

Thus, by the end of the ancient period in Japan in the twelfth century, sushi had grown into a commodity that was sold and found on the banquet tables of the elite. That it was made with lactic-acid fermentation seems very probable. That it was a rice dish is less certain. Rice and sushi are more firmly linked in medieval sushi recipes, examined in the next chapter.

TWO
SUSHI IN THE MEDIEVAL AGE

One of the lingering questions about ancient forms of sushi in China and Japan is the extent to which these depended solely on rice or were made from other grains such as millet, but the use of rice becomes easier to establish for medieval Japan, the period from the late twelfth through to the sixteenth centuries. Medieval sources suggest new forms of sushi in which the rice was meant to be consumed with the fish. In other words, rather than use rice or another grain solely as a medium for fermentation, allowing it to become an odorous porridge that the author of the story in *Tales of Times Now Past* compared to vomit, which was discarded and not consumed, the rice in medieval sushi was made more palatable by virtue of the fact that the sushi was not fermented for so long. Thus, in the medieval age, sushi transitioned from being a preserved food into a dish in which the rice and fish complemented one another, although sushi made with grains besides rice still survive as local foods in some parts of Japan. Unfortunately, the full details of this transformation in sushi-making are not discoverable from the extant sources.

Among the sources that mention sushi in passing are medieval culinary texts written to guide the creation of the banquet cuisine of the warrior and imperial elite. One of these seven existing texts, the anonymous *Shijō School Text on Food Preparation* (Shijōryū hōchōsho), dated to 1489, indicates that sushi is synonymous with sweetfish, but that other types of sushi could be made.[1] These medieval culinary texts indicate that sushi was not commonly served at medieval banquets, or if it was, the dish did not have a special significance. Other records reveal a wide variety of medieval sushi, some of which used vegetables instead of fish.

However, the chefs who wrote these culinary texts made other indirect but lasting contributions to the development of sushi. Known as 'masters of the carving knife' (hōchōnin), they served the elite in Kyoto as chefs from the fourteenth century. With the nearest ocean port in Wakasa Bay more than a day's walk away, the knife masters could not depend on fresh seafood to create elaborate banquets, so they instead made presentation the foremost element in their cuisine, devising complex rules concerning how certain foods were to be served and to whom. Carving well was another of the hallmarks of their status, and they demonstrated their skills in special cutting rituals at banquets, filleting game fowl and fish into inedible sculptures as a form of visual entertainment for guests. Their skills in slicing were equally manifest in the foods they served, particularly in their fish dishes, including a medieval innovation they called sashimi.

RICE SUSHI

Why did people during the medieval period begin to eat rice along with their fermented sushi? Rice, it should be remembered, was used for tribute payments, serving as a currency in

Modern Japanese sashimi knife.

an economy that relied on imported coins and barter instead of a domestically minted currency, and that further enhanced the value of rice as a medium of exchange. Discarding the rice made from sushi-making would have been wasteful and that reason alone may have prompted some to try to eat the rice before it had soured in the process of fermenting the fish. Rice production also increased in the fourteenth century, so people who had formerly made sushi from other grains could potentially now have greater access to rice to use for sushi.[2]

Sushi that has not undergone full lactic-acid fermentation is called 'fresh matured sushi' (namanare), a term that first appears in a fifteenth-century diary of the warrior official Ninagawa Chikamoto (1433–1488).[3] 'Fully fermented sushi' (narezushi), as described in the previous chapter, relies only on salt and grain for its lactic-acid fermentation. In the early modern period, some namanare recipes call for sake or vinegar to speed the fermentation process. However, in the medieval period, 'namanare' referred to sushi made with rice and grain that was meant to be consumed before it had fermented fully,

Pacific saury (*sanma*) namanare.

which meant that sushi was ready in weeks as opposed to months or years.

Eating the sushi before it has fully fermented means that namanare lacks the full sour profile of narezushi. Shingu, a city on the coast in Wakayama Prefecture, is noted for its namanare made from sweetfish, mackerel and pacific saury.[4] Pacific saury runs along the Wakayama coast in November and December. The fish are cleaned and then salted, and after a month they can be made into namanare. The salted fish is first washed and then packed with rice and placed in a pickling barrel with more rice. The chef then adds a layer of leaves before adding another layer of fish and rice to the barrel. A weight is placed on the lid, and the sushi is ready in a month. Pacific saury namanare is sliced when served and the slices are placed against one another to recreate the shape of the fish. Both the fish and rice retain their original taste, although the mouthfeel of the rice is that it's overcooked. It has a mild Cheddar cheese aftertaste. The fish is

FRESH MATURED (NAMANARE) SUSHI

Recipes for 'fresh matured sushi' (namanare) sushi that appear in the medieval period in Japan reduce the fermentation time. The following recipe is an early modern version from the *Collected Writings on Cuisine and an Outline on Seasonings* (Ryōri mōmoku chōmishō), a cookbook by Shōsekiken Sōken published in 1730.

Remove the bones from fish like crucian carp and chub mackerel, or debone [smaller] striped mullet measuring about 20 centimetres [8 in.] and wash well. Cover liberally with aged sake; let rest overnight; then remove the fish and dry. Stuff the abdomens with salted rice. Wrap in bamboo leaves like the kind used for wrapping confectionery and arrange in a bucket. Press salted rice into the gaps [between the fish] and cover with a weighted lid. The sushi will be ready in three or four days in the spring or two days in the summer.[5]

ONE NIGHT SUSHI

Clean a sweetfish and stuff it with cooked grain that is salted more than usual. Wrap it in bamboo grass and light a fire outdoors. Toast the grass wrapping, then wrap it two or three times with a reed tie. Place it on top of the fire, and place a heavy stone on it firmly. One could also tie the wrapped fish firmly to a pillar. It will ferment overnight except if a salted fish is used.[6]

Kokerazushi and 'whole sushi' (sugatazushi, referred to in the text as maruzushi) from *The Amateur Chef* (*Shirōto hōchō*, 1820).

not at all salty, so it can be dipped in soy sauce flavoured with a dash of seven-spice chilli powder (*shichimi tōgarashi*).

The earliest recipe for a namanare sushi is in the *Tales of Cookery* (*Ryōri monogatari*), Japan's first printed cookbook, dated to 1643. Published in the first century of the early modern period, *Tales of Cookery* expresses medieval taste preferences of the fifteenth and sixteenth centuries.[7] The recipe for namanare in *Tales of Cookery* is called One Night Sushi. Contrary to the directions, the fish would not 'ferment overnight', but the taste of the fish would certainly permeate the rice. The recipe attempts to use heat and pressure to replicate the savoury taste of namanare.

The medieval diary cited earlier, *Chikamoto nikki*, which contains the first instance of the word namanare, also mentions 'shingle sushi' (*kokerazushi*), a type of sushi in which slices of fish are placed on top of rice. The second of the two recipes for sushi in *Tales of Cookery* is for shingle sushi.[8]

SHINGLE SUSHI

Fillet a salmon into large slices.
Arrange it on top of salted rice, and press on top.[9]

Like the recipe for namanare, this is a dish for enjoying fresh fish with rice. It is not a fermented food, and it seems to be a predecessor to the scattered sushi (*chirashizushi*) that features a variety of ingredients mixed in and placed on top of sushi rice. The fact that the recipe directs the fish to be pressed on the rice suggests that shingle sushi is also a forerunner of box sushi (*hakozushi*), in which sushi ingredients are placed together inside a lidded box and then formed together by applying pressure with the lid. Nigirizushi, an innovation of the early modern period, simply requires pressing the fish on the rice by hand, and that

PERSIMMON LEAF SUSHI

(2 servings)

Persimmon leaf sushi (*kakinohazushi*) is a type of box sushi (ha-kozushi), which developed from the medieval shingle sushi (kokerazushi) mentioned in this chapter. Persimmon leaf sushi is a local speciality in Nara Prefecture, where it is traditionally made with mackerel. In Japan many different types of leaves were once used to wrap food in order to preserve it, make it portable and add subtle notes of flavour. Persimmon leaves will not affect the taste of this sushi, but they are rich in polyphenol, which helps preserve the fish, and the leaves prevent the rice from drying out.

Commercial makers of persimmon leaf sushi preserve the leaves in salt, so that they can have a year-round supply. This recipe uses fresh American persimmon leaves collected from wild trees. Persimmon leaves can also make an excellent tea when steamed and pan-fried. When gathering wild plants, make sure that they are from an unpolluted area.

This recipe requires a sushi-making box. I use a small wooden rectangular one with a floating lid and a removable bottom. Mine measures 9 × 4 × 2 in. (23 × 10 × 5 cm). A different container can also be used, as long as you can devise a way to press the sushi without flattening it completely, and remove it.

---

1 cup (240 ml) cooked short-grain rice
2 teaspoons vinegar (rice or apple cider vinegar preferred)
1 teaspoon sugar
½ teaspoon salt
3 oz (85 g) or 1 small package of smoked salmon
6 to 10 large persimmon leaves, or enough to wrap the
sushi as described below

Mix the vinegar, sugar and salt in a large bowl. Transfer the cooked rice while hot into the vinegar mixture. Mix it gently. Let it rest for 30 minutes to cool to room temperature.

Make small oblong balls of rice as if you were making nigirizushi and top each with a sliver of salmon. Wrap the sushi in a persimmon leaf and place it in the box. Repeat until the box is full. Put on the floating lid and place a heavy object on top. (A large cantaloupe or pineapple works well for that). Let the sushi press for thirty minutes to an hour.

The sushi can be served unwrapped on top of a persimmon leaf or still wrapped up in one. Although the leaves are high in vitamin C, they are not meant to be eaten.

Persimmon leaf sushi (kakinohazushi).

may be the method used for the recipe for shingle sushi here since no other tools are mentioned.

Besides these innovations, medieval sources mention a wide variety of ingredients used for sushi. A collection of records dating from 1477 to 1600 compiled by women in charge of the office of household affairs for the imperial court mentions sushi 204 times, with varieties including sea bream, eel, crucian carp and sweetfish, as well as vegetarian sushi made from aubergine (eggplant) and bamboo shoots. Records in the late sixteenth century associated with Tanmon'in, a branch of Kōfukuji Temple in Nara, mention sushi made from daikon radish, aubergine and myoga. Missing from this list and from other medieval sources are sushi frequent in ancient texts made from abalone, sea squirts and mussels, along with boar and deer sushi. Rabbit, deer, boar and even bear sushi persisted until the twentieth century in some parts of Japan, but in the medieval period they seem to have dropped off the tables of the elite, who favoured game fowl and fish instead.[10] In sum, medieval sources reveal the variety of sushi available in some circles, but they do not yield many clues about how the sushi were made and how widely they were consumed.

THE SKILLS OF THE MASTERS OF THE CARVING KNIFE

Modern sushi depends on the skills of a chef capable of slicing fish correctly and presenting it attractively, and in the medieval period, carving and presentation became recognized art forms. Chefs were literally 'masters of the carving knife' (hōchōnin) and they were responsible for preparing elaborate banquets consisting of multiple trays of food served simultaneously to high-ranking samurai and aristocrats. Depending on the status of the diner, each tray held a hot or cold soup and a number of

'Master of the Knife' (hōchōnin) (on the right), from *Poetry Contest by Various Artisans* (*Shokunin zukushi uta-awase*, c. 1500, this edition 1769).

side dishes: grilled game fowl or fish, foods served in vinegar dressings and simmered dishes, among others. The main tray, placed directly in front of the diner, contained rice, pickles, condiments such as salt, and chopsticks. Two, four, six or more additional trays were served to the sides of and beyond that main tray, according to the rank of the guest.

Many of these dishes at such a banquet were rich in symbolic meanings, offering clues that helped to differentiate the rank of the guests while showcasing the culinary authority of the chefs. Even a single fish's fin, if placed on a platter, could have tremendous portent. The *Shijō School Text on Food Preparation* details in its instructions how to serve a dish with the anal fin, the fin located at the bottom of the fish near the tail.

It is long been noted that the anal fin is the one that is most highly prized. There are many names for this fin, but in the Shijō school it is important to note that it is called the noble's fin or the cypress needle fin. This is an extremely esoteric teaching, and one that should remain completely secret. Utmost care must be exercised in placing a noble's fin or cypress needle fin on top of a serving of food. The emperor, the shoguns of Kamakura or Kyoto, and the imperial regents should be served in the same manner. A fin might seem innocuous, but much depends on how it is placed on a plate, so if it is out of place, that would be offensive; consequently, refer to the writings about this, although the particulars are restricted to oral teachings. In any case, this fin is eaten by hand, and it must be able to be consumed completely. It is inappropriate to not eat it and simply move it to the side of the plate and ignore it. Serving it takes great care with how it is displayed on the plate, so one must plate it with absolute purity in their hearts. That being the case when someone partakes of something arranged in such a way, they should say 'I am unworthy of this', offering their appreciation to the host, although these days no one upholds such high manners fitting to this as in the past. And, no one even knows the proper way to eat it, except only for the practitioners of our art. Today, people are served so much food that is the only thing that they are thankful for. It is conditions such as these that have led to the gradual decline of our art.[11]

Perhaps the anonymous author's impetus for writing the *Shijō School Text on Food Preparation* was to prevent such instructions about serving food from disappearing. On the one hand, recording such knowledge helped to preserve it so that it could be provided to select disciples. On the other, by affirming that higher teachings were only available through oral instructions, the author ensured that textual authority only enhanced their own personal authority, a strategy typical of medieval secret writings on food and other disciplines. Like other medieval performing arts, hōchōnin organized themselves into schools with their own preferences and styles that they recorded in secret culinary writings meant only for initiates. Several of these schools traced their lineages back to illustrious ancestors. The Shijō, for instance, claimed their family line stemmed from the northern Fujiwara house in the ninth century, the dominant ruling house of that age.

Included with many banquets would be inedible culinary displays equivalent to the French *pièces montées*, sculptures of spun sugar and nougat as found in the *grande cuisine* of Marie-Antoine Carême (1784–1833). Instead of sugar and nougat, hōchōnin fashioned lobster in the shape of boats, placed the heads of snipe in aubergines and presented cooked game fowl with their plumage reattached and posed as if they might fly away.[12] For the latter, *Culinary Text (Ryōri no sho)*, dated to 1573, provides guidelines to display birds that had been taken by hawking. By displaying the game birds in this manner, the chefs called attention to the hunting skills of their employer, the host of the banquet.

> The serving style varies by the four seasons. Place the head of the bird upright in the spring and summer and serve it so that it appears that it will fly away. The head should be down in the autumn and winter, giving it the appearance that it has landed by chance.[13]

Although the meat of these displays would be cooked, by convention they were not consumed, and instead were eaten by the eyes alone.

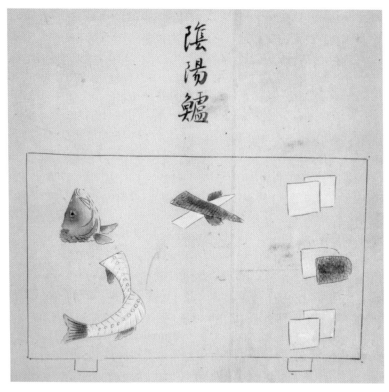

Miyazaki Shikin, 'Ikama School Technique for Preparing a Sea Bass', 1799, detail from watercolour handscroll.

The masters of the carving knife also showcased their skills at elaborate knife ceremonies (hōchō shiki, shikibōchō) in which they filleted a fish or game bird into a pattern forming a flesh sculpture. The ritual was a banquet–entertainment in which a small audience could witness the chef's skill in carving with a long knife and metal chopsticks. It also warded against any bad karma from consuming animal flesh, because the ceremony was supposed to liberate the spirit of the fish or bird and send it to paradise, thereby absolving the person who ate it from the karmic ramifications of consuming the animal.[14]

When the masters of the carving knife turned their attention to preparing banquets, they always included a dish called a *namasu*, made from sliced fish dressed with vinegar. The *Shijō School Text on Food Preparation* indicates a namasu had to have a prominent place at a banquet, and for that reason the namasu was always placed on the main tray at a multi-tray banquet.[15] *Transcript of the Knife* (Hōchō kikigaki), a culinary treatise from the second part of the sixteenth century, provides ten recipes for namasu, including snow namasu, in which daikon is grated over slices of fish; ginger namasu, made in the same way but with grated ginger added; and river raft namasu, pieces of sweetfish arranged on willow leaves to resemble a small boat.[16] In the ancient period, according to the eighth-century poetry compilation *Collection of Myriad Leaves* (Man'yōshū), deer liver was also used for namasu, but raw meat namasu were unknown at medieval banquets.[17]

SASHIMI

A namasu is made from sliced fish and other ingredients, but when the sliced fish is served by itself it is called sashimi, a term that first appears in 1448; however, that is probably not the first time someone in Japan ate raw fish.[18] Archaeological excavations of toilets from the eighth century reveal parasites carried by carp and crucian carp, indicating that those fish had not been cooked before they were served.[19] The word 'sashimi' is probably derived from the term 'cut fish' (kirimi), but cutting had negative connotations in Japanese culture, so the euphemism 'something created' (otsukuri) and the word 'sashimi' were coined instead.[20] A year after the word 'sashimi' appears in a diary, it can also be found in the *Shijō School Text on Food Preparation*, which provides special rules for serving different types of sashimi.

Shark sashimi, for example, required a special arrangement using a fin to differentiate it from other types of fish:

> When making sashimi from shark (*fuka*), make sure to stand the fin upright. This fin had a special name at one time, 'grey hair'. It is not permissible in our style of food preparation to arrange the fins of other fish this way. It is especially inappropriate to display the fins of seabass in this manner. Given that it is improper to serve seabass in this manner these days, it is all the more inappropriate to display lesser fish like carp and crucian carp in that manner.[21]

Fuka designates large sharks, so displaying the sliced fish differently was intended to draw the guests' attention to the fact that something special was being served. Shark sashimi would have had to be served very fresh because shark takes on an ammonia-like smell soon after it is cut, which is the reason why it is generally not served raw even today. However, medieval shark sashimi might have been a type of naturally fermented food similar to the Korean *Hongeo-hoe*, the riceless sushi called osprey sushi in Japan.

Another reason why shark sashimi deserved special attention was that it was from the ocean. The *Shijō School Text on Food Preparation* ranks fish from the ocean above those from rivers, although it makes exceptions for carp and crucian carp, which the author judged superior to most ocean fish. This culinary text indicates that carp and sea bream sashimi were to be served on a bed of cypress leaves. Additionally, sea bream sashimi should be served with the tail cut into three or five pieces accompanied by the boiled internal organs, a method that was apparently a speciality of the Shijō school. All of these different ways of serving sashimi served as visual cues from which the diner could

A serving of sashimi with perilla leaves (shiso).

discern the variety of fish being served. Birds, such as pheasants, were also prepared as sashimi, although in the summertime the Shijō School Text on Food Preparation advised first boiling the meats and then pulling them apart by hand to serve them with vinegar mixed with water pepper (tade).[22] The Culinary Text (Ryōri no sho) provides similar directions for its version of shark sashimi, advising the chef to put the meat in boiling water to bring out the colour of the flesh. Whereas the Shijō School Text on Food Preparation prefers serving cuts of sashimi separately, the Culinary Text directs the reader to serve two different types of sashimi in small piles on the same plate accompanied by two different dipping sauces made from vinegar appropriate to the season.[23]

Medieval preferences for serving sashimi with sauces made from vinegar are particularly noteworthy. The Shijō School Text on Food Preparation recommends wasabi and vinegar for carp, ginger vinegar for sea bream, water pepper vinegar for sea bass, pepper with vinegar for shark and skate, and vinegar with miso for flounder. Besides these dipping sauces, the text notes that a particular

Utagawa Hiroshige, *Sea Bass (Suzuki) and Alfonsino (Kinmedai)*, c. 1832, woodblock print.

characteristic of the Shijō school is to serve sashimi with a dish of salt and some wasabi.[24] The *Culinary Text* reminds the chef to think carefully about which sauces to use and notes the necessity of oral instructions in the matter.[25] Soy sauce would not become the preferred accompaniment to sashimi until the early nineteenth century, when it became more widely used for cooking in general, replacing miso as the preferred flavouring in urban areas.[26] At that point sashimi became more widely consumed in areas where fresh fish and soy sauce were readily available.[27]

If another dish in the hōchōnin's repertoire was not the precursor to sushi rolls (makizushi), it at least shows the same sort of inspiration. Even today, konbu (kelp) is sometimes used in different local sushi recipes such as in Kōchi Prefecture as a substitute for nori to wrap makizushi. In this medieval recipe from *Culinary Text*, the konbu rolls wrap up a fish paste that can be served alone or added to a soup.

Kitagawa Utamaro, *Women Preparing Sashimi*, 1806–20, woodblock print.

KONBU ROLLS

Wash the konbu well and flatten it. Pound raw fish into a paste as you would a recipe for fishcake, add a little finely ground glutinous rice flour, and dilute this mix with a dash of sake. Use a spatula to spread it on the konbu. After it has dried, roll up the konbu and tie it with a rice stalk. Boil these; and after they have boiled sufficiently, remove them to cool before cutting them and serving. For a warm soup, one can boil these in miso and water and serve. There are important oral instructions as well.[28]

The recipe here is closer to a fish sausage than a sushi roll, but it shows the hōchōnin's inventiveness – and that the author had more secrets that could only be told to close associates.

By the late seventeenth century, sashimi eventually replaced namasu as the focal point of high dining, and ocean fish such as sea bream and skipjack tuna were more widely esteemed than carp, crucian carp and other freshwater varieties.[29] One of the contributing factors to these developments was the growth of the commercial fishing industry in the early modern period, which brought fresh fish to Edo (Tokyo). Unlike the landlocked medieval capital of Kyoto, Edo was situated on a bay, and it became Japan's most populous city in that age. Edo was also where the most important developments in sushi history occurred in the early modern period, as the next chapter examines.

THREE
COOKBOOKS AND STREET FOOD: SUSHI IN THE EARLY MODERN ERA

The early modern period (1600–1868) was a golden age for sushi innovation. Published culinary texts of the period, which number almost two hundred different titles, helped to disseminate new ways of making sushi that used sake, vinegar or other additives to hasten the fermentation process. Fermentation in this context did not mean the narezushi created over months or years using lactic-acid fermentation, but rather a combination of fish processed with flavoured rice so as to change the taste of both. Entrepreneurs developed new ways to combine fish and rice as sushi.

This chapter surveys two early modern cookbooks with the most extensive collections of sushi recipes, one from the late seventeenth century and the other from the early nineteenth century, in order to provide insight into sushi-making in the early modern period. Cookery writing from this era is important, for it offers the first recipes for sushi in Japan, but some of the most epochal innovations in early modern sushi were not recorded. Hand-pressed nigirizushi was never mentioned in any early modern cookbook, but it became a popular street food in the early nineteenth century and is now arguably the most familiar form of sushi today. Thus, besides the sushi written about in cookbooks, which helped perfect long-standing techniques, entrepreneurs introduced new forms of quickly made sushi for sale as street foods that eventually found their way into restaurants.

SUSHI IN EARLY MODERN CULINARY BOOKS

Medieval culinary texts served as aides-memoires for professional chefs, the 'masters of the carving knife', in charge of creating banquets for the military and imperial elite; and while some early modern cookbooks contained similar content, the print revolution that occurred in Japan at the turn of the seventeenth century allowed more people greater access to information and changed the character of culinary writing. Early modern texts reflect a transformation in the nature of culinary writing from a private manuscript tradition shared among professionals who adhered to the same aesthetic customs into a much more open genre of writings that not only disseminated the trade secrets of professional chefs but provided new means to represent culinary knowledge to a wider public. The dissemination of culinary knowhow grew with the spread of literacy. At the beginning of the period, some 10 per cent of the population were literate, but in the mid-nineteenth century 40 per cent of boys and 10 per cent of girls received some form of formal education.[1]

Broadly speaking, there were two major forms of culinary text published in the early modern period. The first were recipe collections that showed various ways to prepare different ingredients; the second provided sample menus for banquets that described how to compose a meal for special occasions. Both genres shared a focus on dishes for special events, and

Fish peddler, Meiji period. The ability to make sushi depended on access to fresh fish, which was a rarity for many communities even a few miles from the coast until after the Second World War.

both were written with the male reader in mind. Few cookbooks provide concrete directions on how to prepare rice, and almost none gave recipes for the grain and vegetable porridges that were the main fare for most of the population. In other words, cookbooks were a form of aspirational literature offering a view of the potential of food and how to turn it into a cuisine. Cookbook writers were often less concerned with directing their readers to actually be able to prepare the dishes set forth in their publications, because such menial tasks were meant to be delegated to someone else.

Notwithstanding these developments, only about a dozen early modern texts contain recipes for sushi, and there are several reasons for this. First, most culinary texts focused on banquet cuisine and sushi was never a set feature at banquets, which

Utagawa Hiroshige, *Bowl of Sushi*, c. 1830, woodblock print.

required a variety of soups, simmered and grilled dishes, pickles and a namasu fish salad or sashimi instead. Although from the mid-eighteenth century some restaurants began offering sushi, sushi was dispensable in the planning of most elaborate meals.[2] The second reason why only a few cookbooks mentioned sushi was due to the fact that it was troublesome – not to mention usually malodorous – to make. Most households preserved vegetables as pickles, but a barrel of sushi required much more extensive investment in time and resources, including rice as well as a store of fish. It was easier to purchase sushi, which leads to the third reason why sushi does not appear in most early modern cookbooks: because it was commercially available. In fact, what would become the most widely consumed form of sushi, the hand-formed nigirizushi, is not documented in any early modern cookbook because it was a commercial food, not one typically prepared at home. The author of *An Assemblage of Noted Grain Dishes* (Meihan burui), published in 1802, prefaced his own collection of 33 sushi recipes by stating that sushi was a commercial food and so the only reason to write about it was to allow readers to identify different versions when they purchased them.[3]

SUSHI RECIPES AT THE END OF THE SEVENTEENTH CENTURY

The anonymous *Assembly of Standard Cooking Writings* (Gōrui nichiyō ryōrishō), published in five volumes in 1689, was one of the earliest definitive culinary reference books due to its extensive range of recipes for making alcoholic drinks, miso, soy sauce, confectionery, noodles and pickles. The text even included medical advice such as how to cure blowfish poisoning by drinking a tea made from powdered white butterflies and wood sorrel.[4] However, *Assembly of Standard Cooking Writings* is most revelatory as an expression of the state of sushi-making at the end of the seventeenth century. It includes nine sushi recipes, and I have indicated their variety after the name in brackets.

Sendai-style salmon sushi (hayazushi using sake and sake lees)
sweetfish sushi pickled à la Mino (narezushi)
whitebait sushi (possibly namanare?)
eel sushi (hayazushi using sake)
The funazushi of Gōshū (narezushi)
fast funazushi (hayazushi using sake and vinegar)
salmon sushi, prepared the long way (narezushi)
salmon and roe sushi (hayazushi using sake lees)
sea bream sushi (hayazushi using sake lees)

FAST FUNAZUSHI

Add 540 millilitres [2¼ cups] of salt to 1.8 litres [7½ cups] of sake and simmer; then add 180 millilitres [¾ cup] of vinegar. The vinegar is unnecessary if one plans to ferment the sushi for four or five days. Blend together the sake with grain that has cooled, flavouring it so that it is saltier than one might flavour rice.

Salt the crucian carp, allow them to rest for around two hours, and then wash them quickly. Pack the fish with the prepared rice. This will be ready in about two days, but it is fine to leave it for four or five days.

Make the rice saltier than if you are making namanare. When pressing it [inside a barrel with a weighted lid] increase the weight after four hours, gradually making the weight press down harder.[5]

Of the text's nine recipes, three are for the old-fashioned method of lactic-acid sushi (narezushi), as exemplified by 'The Funazushi of Gōshū', translated in the Introduction. These recipes use only fish, salt and rice. The recipe for whitebait sushi uses the same ingredients, but with the notation that it 'doesn't last long', which might suggest that it is best eaten before it has undergone full fermentation; in other words, it is a 'fresh matured sushi' (namanare), a method that developed in the medieval period, as the last chapter examined.

However, the main innovations in sushi-making found in the remaining recipes are ones that use sake, the lees from sake-making (sake no kasu) or vinegar to create what the text calls 'fast sushi' (hayazushi) by virtue of the fact that these liquids speed the fermentation process. Vinegar alone would become the standard ingredient for making 'fast sushi' such as nigirizushi and makizushi, but Assembly of Standard Cooking Writings demonstrates that the orthodox way to make faster sushi had yet to be determined and therefore offers readers various techniques, several of which are still found in use in local sushi in Japan today.[6] The recipe for fast funazushi (funa no hayazushi) provides an idea about how these new ingredients were to be used.

The recipe relies upon the same tools that would be used to make sushi with lactic-acid fermentation, so the author did not think it necessary to mention having a barrel with a floating lid with a weight stone on top. The recipe directs the reader to increase the weight on the top of the barrel gradually as a way to remove moisture from the sushi. The extra salt might be intended to compensate for the sake and vinegar. Sake was a new ingredient for Japanese sushi, but can be found in the oldest Chinese sushi recipe from the sixth-century *The Important Arts for the People's Welfare* (see Chapter One).

SEA BREAM SUSHI

Combine 3.6 litres [15 cups] of salt with 1.8 litres [7½ cups] of water and boil this mixture of 5.4 litres [22½ cups] down to 3.6 litres [15 cups]; allow this to cool completely.

Cut a sea bream into three filets and place it in the brine; cover with a weighted lid and allow to rest for two days. On the third day, cook 1.8 litres [7½ cups] of brown rice and mix in 1.8 litres [7½ cups] of sake lees. Pack the sea bream with the rice carefully so that the fish do not touch one another. Salted salmon can also be used, but be sure to reduce the salt in the rice; otherwise follow the directions for making the sushi.[7]

Besides sake, *Assembly of Standard Cooking Writings* contains a recipe for sea bream sushi using the lees left over from sake making. The lees are the fermented rice mash from which sake is squeezed out. Sake lees are often used in pickling vegetables, so the inspiration for the recipe for sea bream sushi may have come from there.

The sake-making industry entered into a boom period in the early modern era, meaning that sake lees would have been more widely available and could be put to various culinary uses.

MEIHAN BURUI, A LENS ON SUSHI IN THE NINETEENTH CENTURY

As noted earlier, by the beginning of the nineteenth century, vinegar had become the preferred method for making quick sushi, and *The Assemblage of Noted Grain Dishes* (Meihan burui), an encyclopaedia of methods for preparing various grain foods published in 1802, provides a minnow sushi recipe using vinegar among its 33 different sushi recipes.

MINNOW SUSHI

Mix a little salt with vinegar. Wash the minnows quickly, and let them rest in a strainer. Place rice in a bucket as usual and then arrange the minnows on top. Sprinkle the vinegar over them and place more rice; repeat these steps several times. This is ready to eat in one day.[8]

Utagawa Kunisada and Utagawa Hiroshige, *The En'entei Restaurant: (Actor Suketakaya Takasuke III as) Nagoya Sanza*, from the series 'Famous Restaurants of the Eastern Capital', 1853, woodblock print.

Assemblage of Noted Grain Dishes provides a variety of sushi recipes divided into two sections depending on whether the fish is cut into fillets or served as 'whole sushi' (*maruzushi*, also called *sugatazushi*), indicating that the entire fish is to be used.

Sushi Recipes in *Assemblage of Noted Grain Dishes* by Variety

TYPE	NAME
pressed sushi	shingle sushi
	digging sushi
	lucky scoop
	cherry sushi
	eel sushi
sushi roll	norimakizushi
	wakame rolls
	omelette rolls
	bamboo bark rolls
	tea napkin rolls
vegetarian	matsutake sushi
	bamboo shoot sushi
other	warm sushi
	tofu lees sushi
whole sushi	mackerel sushi
	young stripped mullet sushi
	silver pomfret sushi
	small horse mackerel sushi
	adolescent stripped mullet sushi
	small stripped mullet sushi
	small sea bream sushi
	minnow sushi
	Ōmi-style minnow sushi

whole sushi (continued)	funazushi
	Ōmi-style funazushi
	sardine sushi
	sand borer sushi
	sweetfish sushi
	bucket sushi from Yoshino
	cockle sushi
	Satsuma-style sushi
	Imai-style mackerel sushi
	osprey sushi

The division between 'sushi' and 'whole sushi' in the *Assemblage of Noted Grain Dishes* does not capture all of the variety of sushi described in the text. Some of these innovations would later become sushi favourites, including varieties that the author identifies as commercially available sushi: shingle sushi (koker-azushi), hot sushi and various rolled sushi. It seems the author wanted to present recipes of these sushi so that readers could identify them, and perhaps even try making them at home.

Shingle sushi was a form of pressed sushi eaten since the medieval period. The previous chapter included a recipe for a version with salmon. *Assemblage of Noted Grain Dishes* offers readers the choice of making a luxurious variation of shingle sushi with sea bream, abalone and seepweed (*matsuna*, *Suaeda asparagoides*) or one with somewhat less gourmet ingredients: cockles, tree ears, chestnuts, fried egg, bamboo shoots, shiitake and trefoil. For both versions, the ingredients are placed in a container lined with bamboo bark in alternating layers with cooled rice that has been mixed with vinegar.[9] An aged sake is then sprinkled on top and the container covered with a layer of bamboo bark followed by a lid and a weight stone. The sushi is pressed until it has bonded together and can be cut with a

Meharizushi, sushi made from mustard greens and rice that is often served warm.

knife. The author recommends serving shingle sushi with water pepper, Japanese pepper or ginger on the side. A variation called digging sushi directs the reader to cut the ingredients into small pieces that can be dug out of the barrel with a spoon or chopsticks. The author does not provide the directions for lucky scoop sushi, explaining that it is a product sold by a shop in Osaka, and that the auspicious name is the most special thing about it. The name suggests that some special ingredients were hidden in the mixture and could be found in a lucky spoonful. The other versions of pressed sushi take their names from their ingredients. Cherry sushi is made with octopus, which turns red like a cherry blossom when it is boiled.[10] When shingle sushi is made in a small box whose lid presses the contents together, it is called box sushi (hakozushi).

HOT SUSHI

The Assemblage of Noted Grain Dishes (*Meihan burui*) includes a recipe for hot sushi, one of several sushi that the author notes are sold by vendors. Hot sushi was a winter favourite, a variation of shingle sushi described in Chapters Two and Three.

The product that is generally known as Hot Sushi features simmered ingredients placed while they are still hot on top of warm rice. It is made just like shingle sushi, except [the serving container] is wrapped up in a blanket, then served while it is still warm. Some people really enjoy it. However, I thought that 'hot sushi' made this way would adversely affect the taste of the ingredients and that it would spoil even in the middle of winter, offering a taste that I could not imagine would be appealing at all.

One seller of takeout foods told me that there was no special technique to making hot sushi. Simply everyone grows tired of cold food in the dead of winter, so all he has to do is use warm rice with fish and other ingredients, put these together as sushi and offer it to customers. I tried making it this way and when I created it, I thought the taste turned out quite well. For anyone who would want to attempt to make it, it is definitely worth its current fame. The wonderful taste does not spoil or turn bad at all.[11]

Samples of sushi lunches, with makizushi and nigirizushi in the top row and Osaka-style box sushi in the bottom row.

Today, Osaka is famous for box sushi, but in the age of *Assemblage of Noted Grain Dishes* shingle sushi was all the rage there, and one of the establishments most famous for it was the restaurant Fukumoto Sushi, located in Shinsaibashi. According to Kitagawa Kisō (Morisada) (b. 1810), the author of *Morisada's Extensive Notes on Life* (*Morisada mankō*), the shop opened in the 1830s and was famous for piling a layer of fried eggs, abalone and sea bream about 6 mm (¼ in.) thick on top of rice. Customers lined up to purchase shingle sushi and it was so popular it quickly sold out. However, when competitors began offering a similar product, Fukumoto went out of business.[12]

Besides lucky scoop sushi, other sellers appended the name of famous places to their shingle sushi as a way to advertise the quality of their products, and Sugino noted those names in *Assemblage of Noted Grain Dishes*. There is Ogurazushi (from Kyoto), Chigurazushi (Mie Prefecture), Wakasazushi (Fukui) and Yodogawazushi (a river that runs from Lake Biwa through Kyoto to Osaka). These were well-known products, but Sugino explains that their ingredients were not special, and he advised against giving these as gifts even if they were inexpensive.[13] Shingle sushi has largely disappeared in Japan except for regional examples, one of the most famous being the kokerazushi of Muroto in Kōchi Prefecture, which looks like a layer cake decorated with artful strips of mackerel, hijiki, nori and egg.[14]

While Sugino is dismissive of the various place names that sushi sellers have used to market their shingle sushi, his other recipes draw upon the fame of other famous locales: Ōmi for its funazushi and Yoshino in Nara for its sweetfish sushi traditionally served in a container similar in appearance to a well bucket (*tsurube*), therefore earning the name bucket sushi. Satsuma sushi is distinct for its method of preparation. Sugino writes, 'The process for making Satsuma sushi is different from other locales in that it does not use vinegar, but uses sake instead for making sushi.'[15] Imai sushi, named for a locale in Nara, is a variation of mackerel sushi made in one day, which Sugino offers as a variation of his mackerel sushi recipe, which took several days to prepare.[16] On the one hand, his comments provide evidence that vinegar has clearly become the standard for sushi-making in Sugino's time. On the other, Sugino also reveals an acute awareness of regional variations in sushi-making and betrays his knowledge of fish despite living in landlocked Kyoto, as is evident from directions for mackerel sushi.

MACKEREL SUSHI

The most important thing to note is the choice of mackerel. Among mackerel, there are northern and western varieties, and their taste is quite different depending on the places they were caught. While the locations that they were fished are not exactly remote, the northern mackerel (those caught in the areas of Wakasa and Tango), are the ones that have been salted the best. Kumano is well known for its mackerel, but most of the ones that come from that more distant area arrive by boat in summer and come salted on a skewer. Northern mackerel travel a shorter distance overland from Osaka, and the people who make them salt the fish in an amount appropriate for them to arrive preserved. The flesh is still soft and the taste is extraordinary.

As for the western mackerel, most of these come from the Izumo area and the rest are from other places requiring travel by boat over sea routes, so when a storm makes shipping impossible the delay in the number of days of their arrival can go beyond reckoning. Since the distance is so far from here and it becomes problematic to predict the date of the arrival of the fish, they are all heavily salted. Even if they are preserved in a barrel, the flesh becomes hard and dried out, and the taste suffers for it. Consequently, it is best to make sushi only with northern mackerel, albeit that even northern mackerel too should be avoided if they arrived in the summer after too many days travel.[17]

Slow travel and the lack of any refrigeration made knowledge of any fish's origins and local methods of preparation critically important for people like Sugino living in Kyoto. All of the mackerel arrived salted, but those from Wakasa and Tango (modern Fukui and Kyoto Prefectures) would have less salt, since they

Sushi chef making makizushi.

were far closer than the western mackerel from Izumo (modern Shimane Prefecture). Owing to the frequency with which traders took mackerel along the northern route, the road from Kyoto to Wakasa Bay was nicknamed the 'mackerel highway' in the early modern period. Mackerel from Kumano (modern Mie and Wakayama Prefectures) may be famous in their place of origin, but according to Sugino, these took too long to arrive to be much good for sushi-making. Skewered mackerel from Kumano did become a delicacy of the Obon festival in late summer for residents of Kyoto.

The example of shingle sushi shows the extent to which sushi had become a commercial product by the nineteenth century. Sushi historian Hibino Terutoshi has pointed to the records of mercantile establishments that reveal the names of sushi shops as some indication of the growth in the trade. A list compiled in 1687 includes only two sushi shops in Edo, but one about a century later shows twenty or more.[18] However, these lists do not include food stands such as the one that artist Utagawa Hiroshige (1797–1858) portrayed in a festival sometime between 1830 and 1844 (see p. 101). Sushi pushcarts also appeared in Edo in the 1770s.[19]

Makizushi

Shingle sushi may have been a notable food sold outside the home in urban areas at the beginning of the 1800s, but another style of sushi that Sugino included was becoming a commercial success at the time his book was published. Sushi historians date the take-off point for sushi rolls to the latter half the eighteenth century. Hibino Terutoshi narrows that date to 1770–80, based on his interpretation of culinary texts.[20] Kitagawa Kisō (Morisada) described three versions of sushi rolls. One was an omelette stuffed with rice and pieces of nori and dried gourd. The other two were nori rolls with dried gourd stuffing: one was small and tightly wound, and the other large.[21] Because of these meagre ingredients, sushi rolls were inexpensive, at least according to one reference from 1852 which prices one roll at sixteen copper coins (mon), a half-roll at eight and a portion of a roll for four coins.[22] In other words, a sushi roll was an inexpensive street food considering that a bowl of noodles cost sixteen coins and the price for a serving of sweet rice dumplings was four coins.[23]

Just as he provides the gourmet versions of shingle sushi, Sugino's examples of rolled sushi are more sophisticated than the ones Kitagawa described for sale. His recipe for norimak-izushi in *An Assemblage of Noted Grain Dishes* provides the basis for the rest.

> ## ROLLED SUSHI, ALSO CALLED NORIMAKIZUSHI
>
> Spread out Asakusa nori on a cutting board and smear on the rice used for shingle sushi. Use ingredients such as sea bream, abalone, shiitake, trefoil, and red and green perilla leaves. Roll it up tightly and cover with a damp cloth for a time before cutting. If wakame from Kishū is used this is called memakizushi.[24]

Sugino provides a recipe for makizushi similar to the one used today, and he gives two variations: memakizushi, using wakame instead of nori, and one with bamboo bark. The latter is wrapped in bamboo bark, which gives the sushi a rolled shape by virtue of being pressed in a box for several hours. Sugino suggests that it is an ideal travel food, akin to an onigiri rice ball, formed by hand with an umeboshi (pickled apricot) or something else inside. Another variation Sugino suggests is to roll the sushi rice and ingredients up in a thin omelette. When egg whites and yolks are made into separate omelette sushi rolls, Sugino dubs them tea napkin rolls.[25]

Asakusa nori was a variety of seaweed harvested from the Sumida River near Asakusa in Edo, a fortuitous location for sushi history since the area was also home to papermakers. In the first half of the eighteenth century, some of these craftspeople used their papermaking skills to transform nori into flat sheets, a technique that soon spread to other parts of the country. We know the nori-makers of Asakusa did not invent this technique, because it is mentioned in one medieval culinary text dating to the mid-sixteenth century. However, they were the first to commercialize it.[26] Nori began to be used in sushi recipes from the latter half of the eighteenth century, although makizushi recipes using other wrappers, such as blowfish skin and paper, can be found in early modern culinary texts.[27] Yet nori soon became

Inarizushi, makizushi and box sushi (hakozushi) in a train lunch (*ekiben*).

standard for rolled sushi, also called nori rolls (norimaki). From the late nineteenth century, nori became a cultivated crop in Edo Bay and elsewhere. Around the end of the Meiji period in 1912, the custom of toasting the nori before using it to make makizushi developed, but in the Kansai area of Osaka and Kyoto, untoasted dry nori remains common today. Both versions of nori can be found at supermarkets in ready-to-use packs.[28]

Inarizushi

A form of wrapped sushi that Sugino and other early modern cookbook authors omitted was sushi rice in a sheet of fried tofu, a recipe called inarizushi, named after the Inari Shrine in Kyoto, whose deity is served by fox spirits who are said to love tofu. Inarizushi is also called 'fox sushi' (kitsunezushi) in the Kansai area and in places near Japan's Inland Sea. Fans familiar with Kabuki and Bunraku theatres will catch the reference to inarizushi as *Shinodazushi*, recalling the play *A Courtly*

Mirror of Ashiya Dōman (Ashiya Dōman Ōuchi Kagami) about a fox in the Shinoda forest in Osaka Prefecture who turns into a girl. Inarizushi is also referred to as 'fried tofu sushi' (abura'agezushi).[29]

The history of inarizushi is uncertain, but it debuts in the historical record in the first part of the nineteenth century as a street food in Edo. Kitagawa describes the dish as a fried tofu wrapping around rice containing bits of mushroom and dried gourd. Another version sold in Edo around the midpoint of the nineteenth century was a wrapper of fried tofu stuffed with rice or tofu lees and eaten with soy sauce and wasabi.[30] In the Tokyo area today, inarizushi are traditionally rectangular shaped reminiscent of a tawara, the straw bag once used to contain rice. Triangular inarizushi are preferred in the Osaka and Kyoto area.

SHAPED BY HAND 'BEFORE EDO'

Hand-formed nigirizushi, the most important development in sushi history during the early modern period, was also absent from all period cookbooks, and to trace its history we must shift from Sugino's home in Kyoto to Edo, which had, by the mid-eighteenth century, become a toponym for fresh seafood thanks to the proximity of Edo Bay. The phrase 'before Edo' (Edomae) appeared in the first part of the eighteenth century as a reference to local fish, chiefly eel, but also catfish, horse mackerel, sea bream and false halibut, which were sourced in the bay or in Edo's rivers. Eel, served in the cat-tail style (kabayaki), grilled on skewers with a tangy sauce so that they resembled the namesake plant, rose in popularity in the mid-eighteenth century, and the people of Edo favoured the local variety caught in the city's rivers, which they designated Edomae in contrast to the 'eel that had travelled' (tabi unagi) imported from outside the city. Eel shops advertised their Edomae eel dishes, and the term became a brand name.[31] Over time, the term Edomae saw wider application, gradually extending not just to the entirety of Edo Bay but to areas on the coasts of nearby provinces and the seafood of these regions, including abalone, Pacific saury, skipjack tuna and tuna caught, transported and sold in the fish markets of Edo. By the nineteenth century, Edomae referred not just to seafood but the restaurants that sold it and even the culture of the entertainment areas in Edo. Much later, after the Second World War, Edomae came to refer to 'fresh' sushi in the Tokyo style, namely nigirizushi.[32]

Though made famous in Edo, nigirizushi may not have been invented there. Sushi made from rice seasoned with vinegar and formed into an oval by hand with slices of mackerel or cherry salmon on top were a festival food in Kaga in Ishikawa Prefecture before they became popular in early nineteenth-century Edo, according to sushi historian Hibino Terutoshi. In the version made in Kaga, the hand-formed sushi are wrapped in bamboo grass leaves before being placed in a box with a weight on top and left overnight, long enough for the fish and rice to imbue each other with flavour but not too long for anything to spoil or for the rice to harden.[33]

Hanaya Yohe'e (often referred to in English as Hanaya Yohei, 1799–1858) was the person credited with popularizing nigirizushi in Edo, at least according to the story told in a book written by his grandson Koizumi Seizaburō (1884–1950) ninety years later. Koizumi's *How to Make Sushi at Home* (*Katei sushi no tsukekata*), published in 1910, has been read by sushi historians for its insights into what Hanaya Yohe'e created and why. The text indicates that Hanaya did not invent nigirizushi, but instead that he perfected the recipe, solving the mistakes that thwarted his predecessors.[34] Allegedly, Hanaya worked as an apprentice to a moneylender until the age of twenty and had other jobs

Utagawa Hiroshige III, *The Revised Fifty-three Stations: Revised Travel Journal No. 39, Goyu, Tama Sushi Stand at the East Entrance*, from the series 'Famous Places in Tōkai', 1875, woodblock print.

before selling sushi in a cart in Matsuichō in Edo. He eventually established a shop in Ryōgoku around 1825.[35]

Yohe'e's shop and the other sushi restaurants in the period may have just been elaborate food stands. Most of the sushi restaurants in early twentieth-century Tokyo were places where one stood and ate. Consequently, this modern custom was most certainly a practice that had continued from Yohe'e's time.

According to his grandson, Hanaya Yohe'e started off by selling a form of pressed sushi, placing fish slices on rice in a box and putting a lid with a weight on top, allowing it to rest for three or four hours. Pressing the sushi this way allowed it to last for up to three days, but Yohe'e could not make enough sushi on demand for customers by this method. He is also credited with observing how the succulent oils of the fish tended to become lost when the fish was pressed too much.[36]

Yohe'e, in other words, started his career making a form of box sushi, a variety for which Osaka was famous. Kitagawa describes in his *Extensive Notes on Life* that box sushi was a version of shingle sushi made with a square container approximately 20 cm (8 in.) on each side. First, the box was filled halfway with rice flavoured with salt and vinegar. Then shreds of matsutake that had been simmered in vinegar were added, followed by another layer of rice. Above that the chef placed slices of sea bream, abalone and other fish. The top layer would have egg in the middle and tree ears along the sides to form a design of a diamond broken with slices of sea bream or abalone. An entire container of this sold for 64 copper coins with one serving costing four coins, he reported.[37]

Hanaya Yohe'e changed this recipe by not using a box, simply pressing ingredients directly on to small mounds of rice. If the directions in *How to Make Sushi at Home* can be taken as any guide, Hanaya Yohe'e's nigirizushi were massive, weighing some

COOKBOOKS AND STREET FOOD: SUSHI IN THE EARLY MODERN ERA

Meiji-period sushi from Koizumi Seizaburō, *How to Make Sushi at Home* (*Katei sushi no tsukekata*) published in 1910. This image offers an idea of what Yohe'e's sushi might have looked like.

45 g (1½ oz), roughly 2.5 times the size of nigirizushi typically made today. His sushi was also much saltier. The recipe for sushi rice in *How to Make Sushi at Home* calls for 3.6 litres (15 cups) of rice to 180 ml (¾ cup) of vinegar and 180 ml (¾ cup) of salt, about three times more salt than most sushi rice recipes today. Most current sushi rice recipes also add sugar, but not the version in *How to Make Sushi at Home*.

True to the spirit of Edomae, *How to Make Sushi at Home* favours fish from Edo Bay, except bluefin tuna and octopus, which were considered to be low-grade seafood by the author, although both were part of the early modern sushi repertoire of ingredients. Written at a time before home refrigeration, the text's seasonal recommendations for fish were the varieties available: conger eel, half beak, whitebait and bastard halibut for the spring; sand borer, abalone and tiger prawn for early summer;

Sushi at the Sukiyabashi Jirō restaurant in Tokyo, 2019.

conger eel, sweetfish, butterfish and thin nori rolls for autumn;
squid, venus clam, and larger nori rolls for winter. Omelette
sushi could be sold throughout the year. More surprisingly is
the fact that most of these ingredients were seasoned before
being matched with rice. The fish were pickled, blanched in soy
sauce, boiled in mirin or soy sauce, grilled or processed by other
methods. Squid and sandborer were pickled in vinegar; bastard
halibut was blanched in soy sauce and mirin; sweetfish was
salted; conger eel was grilled; shrimp were boiled; and cockles
were briefly marinated in vinegar and soy sauce.[38] Nigirizushi
was by no means raw.

The size and techniques involved in making nigirizushi
help to explain why it could be priced rather high in the early
modern period relative to other foods sold at stands. One
source at the end of the early modern period indicates that
the sushi restaurant Matsuya offered one nigirizushi for 250

copper coins.[39] This must have been the most gourmet version. Kitagawa observed that nigirizushi made from omelette, tiger prawn, whitebait and bluefin tuna cost around eight copper coins and were sold with pickled ginger and water pepper, a long-favoured accompaniment to sashimi. Gizzard shad and bluefin tuna sushi were flavoured with a bit of wasabi between the fish and rice, but not served with soy sauce. Kitagawa further noted that sushi was becoming Edo's most popular food:

> In Edo there are many sushi shops. In each ward there are one or two sushi shops compared to soba shops of which there are only one for every one or two wards. The well-known sushi stores do not operate food stands, but typically others do. There are many independent sushi stands as well.

Kitagawa mentions that Matsu no Sushi (Pine Sushi) is among the most famous sushi establishments in Edo and he also includes a passing nod to Yohe'e Sushi in Ryōgoku. Then there were sushi stands called *yatai*, either operated by sushi restaurants or independently, according to Kitagawa.[40]

Nigirizushi as well as inarizushi and makizushi were the most prominent street foods before Edo took the name Tokyo in 1868.[41] The only other food to compete with sushi was tempura. Both sushi and tempura food stands began around the same time in the 1770s and both catered to the popular market, offering inexpensive foods meant to be eaten as snacks. Customers queued up to these stands, ordered and ate while standing nearby. Tempura stands sold vegetables and fish fried in batter and provided customers with complimentary sauce and grated daikon to dip their tempura in.[42] Tempura worked well as a street food because it required hot oil to prepare, making it troublesome to make at home.

Though they might purchase the aforementioned forms of sushi as a snack, they were not among the dishes that commoners living in Edo prepared for themselves at home, at least if one is judging from one ranking of a hundred favourite dishes for commoners published in the 1830s in a broadsheet intended for a popular audience. Tempura appears just once on this list and sushi is omitted entirely.[43] Sushi became a meal only in the modern period, as the next chapter describes.

FOUR
SUSHI IN MODERN JAPAN, FROM SNACK TO DELICACY

The story of sushi in the modern period, beginning in the late nineteenth century, was less about changes in recipes than the way it was sold. In Tokyo before the Second World War, sushi was a quintessential street food, purchased from a food stand called a yatai and eaten while standing, as in the early modern period. Often the only person seated in a sushi restaurant was the chef; sushi was a snack food. After the war, sushi grew into more of a meal with a standard serving size of ten pieces. Restaurants equipped with conveyor belts bringing plates of sushi to customers became the new inexpensive option for a sushi meal. These restaurants served the sushi 'styles of Edo' – nigirizushi, makizushi and inarizushi – helping to make these synonymous with sushi as a whole throughout Japan in the post-war period, although some regions continued to make their traditional styles of sushi.

FROM FOOD STANDS TO RESTAURANTS

A guide to Tokyo published in 1907 listed only six sushi restaurants in Tokyo, including Yohe'e Sushi in Hongyō; Daikoku, with branches in Asakusa and Shiba (today the southern part of modern Minato Ward); Kenukizushi and Tengu in Nihonbashi; and Tamazushi in Shiba. This makes the number of sushi restaurants almost one-fifth of the number of Western restaurants at the time.[1] However, this guide appears to be focusing only on higher-end sushi places, ignoring the fact that most people in Tokyo purchased sushi from food stands.

One author who did seek to guide readers to the seamier side of Japan, including working-class eateries such as food stands, was Taizo Fujimoto, author of the English book *The Nightside of Japan*. Fujimoto described a sushi stand in the Ginza in this 1915 publication:

> In square boxes covered with glass on the sushi stall several kinds of sushi are arranged in rows – each small oval mass of pickled rice being covered with red flesh of tunny fish, yellow square piece of egg, pink and white flesh of lobster or shrimp, pearl white slice of cuttle fish, silvery flesh of saba fish (*scomber pneumatophorus*), or rolled up with parched laver. Three or four young fellows of clerk form are standing near each of the one dish cooking and the sushi stalls, and those in the former eat cutlet or beef-steak and drink wine; but the lovers of sushi drink tea which emits an agreeable perfume.[2]

Fujimoto informs the reader how 'sushi' – that is to say, nigirizushi and makizushi – were displayed under a glass cover and how the sushi stand appeared to attract a somewhat better class of customer than the young workers eating meat and drinking

Detail of a sushi stand (middle) from Utagawa Hiroshige, *Amusements While Waiting for the Moon on the Night of the Twenty-sixth in Takanawa*, from the series 'Famous Places of the Eastern Capital', 1820s, woodblock print, triptych.

wine (that is, sake) nearby. One reason why sushi stands did not serve alcohol, which must have been a lucrative trade, was that sake drinkers would need a place to sit down and that would require supplying chairs. Sushi stalls did not need pots for oil like tempura stands or braziers to cook beef stew, so they were more portable. Some sushi stands from around the turn of the century were built on wheels.[3]

Koizumi Seizaburō (1884–1950), author of *How to Make Sushi at Home* (*Katei sushi no tsukekata*), published in 1910, draws a distinction between two types of sushi stands. Koizumi claimed in the same publication that his grandfather Hanaya Yohe'e had first operated a sushi stand before perfecting the recipe for nigirizushi and later opening a restaurant that Koizumi himself still owned. Consequently, Koizumi understood the origins of nigirizushi as a street food. But, as a restaurateur, he portrayed his establishment as being far above some sushi stands that he claimed were run by con artists. Legitimate sushi stands were those operated by sushi restaurants, which opened the stands as a way to sell their leftovers at night, offering the same quality of food as one would expect within the restaurant. Koizumi made this observation without acknowledging that the sushi sold at night from a stand would not be as fresh as the sushi made in the restaurant earlier in the day. The less reliable stands, he explained, were the ones not affiliated with a restaurant. They did not carry the same ingredients, relied on less expensive fish and did not even offer shrimp or sea bream, which Koizumi interpreted as owing to the fact that the owners of these stands lacked the capital to buy or rent a restaurant.[4] According to Koizumi, the worst stands offered dubious foods such as bluefin tuna (*maguro*) from Sendai in Miyagi Prefecture, which was in reality dyed tofu. They sold squid that was actually a fishcake called *hanpen*, made from pulverized fish and yam. And they substituted leftover tofu lees for shrimp and claimed that shark was conger eel. Such people lacked both ethics and skills. Koizumi declared: 'an artisan (*shokunin*) who has worked at a food stand or trained at one is inclined toward having slipshod techniques, and none of them can make nigirizushi.'[5]

Koizumi's criticism of the lack of technique of sushi-stand operators shows his bias against them, but also reflects how many of the people who sold sushi at stands may have lacked any formal training. In fact, operating a sushi stand was a trade that was relatively easy to enter, according to the book *Taishō Handbook for Business* (*Taishō eigyō benran*), published in 1914. This book provided information for entrepreneurs wishing to start their own sushi business. It offered basic recipes for nigirizushi and makizushi, indicating that these were the most lucrative types to make. According to the *Taishō Handbook for Business*, one could open a sushi stand for an investment of as little as 15 to 30 yen, not including equipment, which cost an additional 45 yen. This was a considerable amount of capital, considering that a month's tuition at a cooking school in Tokyo at that time was around one-and-a-half yen.[6] However, opening a stand was much less expensive than opening a sushi restaurant, which was 163 yen: 13 to cover the rent, 50 for a deposit to the landlord, 50 for furnishings, 30 for servingware and 20 for miscellaneous expenses. This too was a considerable amount of capital, but far less than starting up a Western restaurant, according to the same book, which could run to between to 230 and 5,000 yen, depending on the quality of the establishment one desired.[7]

MEAT THIN ROLLS

The first cookbook dedicated exclusively to sushi was Koizumi Seizaburō's (1884–1950) *How to Make Sushi at Home* (*Katei sushi no tsukekata*), published in 1910, an authoritative work due to its association with the sushi restaurant started by Koizumi's grandfather, Hanaya Yohe'e, whom many thought invented nigirizushi. Koizumi indicates that the home cook interested in sushi-making should start with rolled sushi (makizushi). Writing in the Meiji period (1868–1912), when many of Japan's elite embraced Western eating habits, including beef and pork consumption, Koizumi included a recipe for a meat sushi, which can be considered an early example of fusion cuisine. The directions refer to the previous recipe for wasabi thin rolls, now called hot iron rolls (*tekkamaki*) for the red colour of the fatty tuna used. As part of the general directions for making thin rolls, Koizumi advises spreading rice evenly on a half sheet of dried nori so that it is about 3 mm (⅛ in.) thick, leaving about a centimetre and a half (½ in.) at the top without rice to allow for a bit of nori to overlap when it is rolled up. The ingredients go into the middle of the rice and then the sushi is rolled up and sliced.[8]

MEAT THIN ROLLS

Dried nori, ham (or another cold meat), black pepper,
sushi rice

Suitable to make at home, this is pleasing and easily made as a meal for an outing.

Follow the directions for wasabi thin rolls [and instead of tuna] use an appropriate amount of meat for the ingredients.

> Whether the choice is ham or another cold meat, follow the
> grain of the meat and slice it thinly as possible, then sprinkle
> a little black pepper on top [before rolling up].[9]

The *Taishō Handbook for Business* sketches out the layout
of a small sushi shop:

> Assuming the frontage is 3.6 metres (4 yd), that would in-
> clude a doorway of 1.8 metres (6 feet) in the middle to hang
> a shop curtain. Place a small bench outside the shop with a
> little window above it for a small stand to display some sushi
> and other things made by the shop as samples. Inside the
> shop, erect a wall to divide the room to create a space for cus-
> tomers and build 61-centimetre (24-in.) wide benches with
> tatami for seating. The [other] room for preparing the sushi
> will have a wood floor with a cooking pot in the corner. The
> arrangements will vary depending on the place you rent.[10]

The fact that the description mentions only that the cooking area should have a wood floor suggests that customers may
have been served in a room with a dirt floor. The description
does not mention if the sushi chef is meant to sit or stand, but
before the Second World War, it was the custom for chefs to sit
on tatami mats and for customers to stand, although by the end
of the Meiji period in 1912, some sushi places did offer seating
perhaps along the lines of the description above. Sitting was so
typical of sushi chefs at that time that the chefs who could stand
up were believed to be those who did not have enough work.[11]

According to the *Taishō Handbook for Business*, a chef could
sell nigirizushi for between 7 and 15 *sen* per serving, with a *sen*
being one-hundredth of a yen. Inarizushi should be priced at
5 *sen*. Based on those prices against expenses and assuming an

adequate customer base, the book estimated a profit of 6 to 13 yen per month.[12] One of the reasons why sushi was a more viable profession at the time this book was published was the greater availability in cities of ice to preserve the fish, which allowed aspiring sushi chefs to maintain their ingredients longer and offer more varied toppings.[13]

Sushi offered economic opportunities but also a competitive marketplace. By one estimate, in 1926 there were some 3,100 sushi restaurants and 800 sushi stands in a city of 6.3 million people.[14] The number of sushi stands might well be an underestimate. The artist Yokoi Kōzō (1889–1965) spent a year documenting the history of stands that sold food and other goods, and in a 1931 publication he estimated that 860 people derived income from these in Asakusa alone, selling foods beyond sushi such as ramen, yakitori, curry rice and beef on rice, as well as a wide range of consumer goods including dolls, clothing, shoes, newspapers, pipes and baseball equipment.[15] Sushi stands, in other words, were part of a much larger culture of street selling and mass culture in Tokyo before the Second World War.

SUSHI STANDS AND RESTAURANTS IN ASAKUSA

The social researcher Ishizumi Harunosuke (1890–1939) offered his analysis of why certain sushi operations succeeded and others failed in the downtown entertainment area of Asakusa in Tokyo in his *Study of the Economics of Asakusa* (*Asakusa keizaigaku*), published in 1933. In it, he traced how the area had become famous for its sushi shops by the 1930s. Ishizumi found that the history of sushi in Asakusa began in the 1870s, and he explained that the first sushi establishment was a shop named Hanai. Hanai was a stand where customers stood and ate, but it gained

Sushi chef.

a positive reputation for its fresh ingredients and the large size of its nigirizushi. Ishizumi explained that the nigirizushi rice and tuna on top at Hanai were so large that the sushi had to be consumed in two or three bites. Hanai, however, did not survive long in the Meiji period (1868–1912), and Ishizumi attributed that to the low margins on its sushi sales and competition from other sushi shops nearby, which had spread in the mid-Meiji years in Asakusa 'like bamboo shoots after a rainstorm'. Some sushi places differentiated themselves by operating at night, but all of them were standing eateries. Sushi in Asakusa could only be conceived as a food that people stood to eat until just before the turn of the century, when a sushi chef named Nagai opened an establishment with tables and chairs; his place became very popular, setting the trend for sushi eateries in the area to offer sit-down service.

Sushi stands also began diversifying their menus by offering tempura, while at the same time small restaurants began selling sushi. By the late Meiji period, even diners and elite restaurants included sushi on their menus and that made the competition among Asakusa's sushi places even fiercer. One of the victors in this struggle was the shop named Bull's Eye (*Janome*) Sushi. Ishizumi told the story of the establishment through the career of its owner, who was born into a family of sushi-makers in Asakusa but trained at a different restaurant in Imagawabashi, becoming the adopted son-in-law there before returning to Asakusa to open a sushi stand called Chin'ya. Chin'ya established a reputation and provided the owner with enough capital to open a sushi restaurant he named Janome. Like the store Hanai before it, Janome and other successful sushi restaurants depended on obtaining the freshest ingredients by visiting the fish market early. Ishizumi advised against eating at any sushi place whose owner went to the fish market in the afternoon.

At some establishments, though, the freshness of the fish hardly mattered because the customers came to see the beautiful female serving staff. Matsu Sushi was one such business, noted more for the owner's three beautiful daughters than for its food, Ishizumi confided. Another way that Asakusa sushi places made money was by selling their leftover rice, and Ishizumi estimated that twenty to thirty people subsisted on this inexpensive food source, most of whom were women.[16] Ishizumi's study ends with a bleak forecast for the future of sushi in Asakusa, observing that

Sushi bar.

the quality of the sushi in the area had declined at the same time that sushi could be found in non-speciality sushi restaurants.

In the 1920s and '30s the ordinary folk who had long patronized the sushi stands in Asakusa and elsewhere in Tokyo were turning to department-store dining rooms, where they could find sushi along with a variety of other Western, Japanese and Chinese dishes at affordable prices.[17] Sushi was on the menu at Shirokiya department store in Tokyo as early as 1904, the year it became the first department store to offer its customers a place to dine. At 15 *sen*, sushi cost less than a sandwich priced at 20 *sen* at Shirokiya in 1911, but more than Western or Japanese desserts that cost 12 and 10 *sen* respectively. Mitsukoshi and Daimaru department stores opened their dining halls in 1907 and 1908 and they too offered sushi, priced at 15 *sen* at Mitsukoshi.[18] Thus, department stores helped move sushi out of the masculine world of the food stand into a setting where women and families felt comfortable dining. The availability of sushi outside of a sushi shop or specialized restaurant did not necessarily mean that traditional sushi-sellers suffered. By 1931 Janome Sushi had shops throughout Tokyo, making it the first sushi chain restaurant.[19] The greater availability of sushi confirmed its status as an inexpensive snack food for everyone.

SUSHI CRITICS

The greater availability of sushi caught the attention of food writers in the 1930s. In contrast to its elevated status today, before the Second World War, sushi, especially the version sold at food stands, was a food that many critics scorned. One of the most prominent food writers at the time was the reporter Matsuzaki Tenmin (1878–1934). In 1906 Matsuzaki moved from Osaka to Tokyo and started working for the *Tokyo Asahi Shimbun* newspaper. From 1928 until his death in 1934, he also wrote for *Culinary Magazine* (Shokudōraku), serving as the publication's editor from 1928 to 1930. *Shokudōraku* took its name from Japan's first gourmet magazine, which ran from 1905 to 1907 and had been inspired by the best-selling gourmet novel of the same title by reporter Murai Gensai (1863–1927). In his guide to eating out in Tokyo, *A Walker's Guide to Eating in Tokyo* (Tōkyō tabearuki) published in 1931, Matsuzaki grouped sushi places alongside soba shops as inexpensive joints that 'catered to the masses', going so far as to include in that group the sushi restaurant Yohe'e, whose founder was credited with perfecting the methods to make nigirizushi.[20] The original Yohe'e restaurant was destroyed in the Tokyo earthquake in 1923, but it reopened in Ryōgoku in 1925 advertising a dining room and a large hall with tatami mats able to seat parties of a hundred.[21] But Matsuzaki reserved harsh words for Yohe'e Sushi, writing:

> There are a great many sushi places in Tokyo, but the ones that are well known by the masses are Yohe'e in Ryōgoku, Shintomizushi in Shinbashi, Sushikiyo in Asakusa . . . Just looking one can see that their sushi are truly thick, and that Yohe'e Sushi and the rest of those places are where one can see such deplorable scenes as young hoodlums stuffing their faces. Even though it's called Tokyo nigirizushi, somehow it seems more like the box sushi of Kamigata. Such a style might make Yohe'e a king, but the taste smacks of the countryside.[22]

Matsuzaki's comparison of Yohe'e's sushi to the pressed sushi of Kamigata, the Osaka area, was due to the fact that 'it tasted like it was pressed too hard.'[23] Matsuzaki had a point. Looking at the recipes in the sushi cookbook written by the owner of Yohe'e, the size of the sushi are approximately two-and-a-half times larger than typical nigirizushi sold today. Yohe'e's sushi would have been much saltier as well because he used about three times more salt to make sushi rice than is used today, and he did not add any sugar, which is standard today.[24] The unsavouriness of the Yohe'e restaurant may also be attributed to the fact that the owner faced eight months in prison for embezzlement in 1931.[25]

While condemning sushi as a mass food, Matsuzaki Tenmin did recommend one sushi place:

At Shintomizushi in Shinbashi the cost is not cheap, but
the owner has the bearings of a child of Edo: he stands at
the ready to work, and one is able to eat very well there. The
ingredients are fresh whether its conger eel, tuna, gizzard
shad, or cockle. Only the absolute best items are used, so
one can safely satisfy oneself. At the food stand called Sail
(Hoka), something priced around 50 sen would cost 80 or 90
sen at Shintomi, but one is able to sense the freshness, and
the goodness feels almost like a fish jumping out of water . . .
Good or bad ingredients, high or low quality rice, the degree
to which the rice is cooked, the firmness or softness of the
way the sushi was pressed together, and the seasoning with
the vinegar all contribute to the taste of the nigirizushi; there
are many factors and these cannot be summarized with a

Sushi bar.

single word but a place like Shintomizushi as an example
of nigirizushi in Tokyo has a taste that never slips below
top rank.[26]

Matsuzaki suggests that Shintomizushi had what writers
before him had referred to as the reason for the success of any
sushi restaurant, namely fresh ingredients, which the chef was
able to use in the best ways possible. Wealthy gourmets like
Matsuzaki could afford to pay 80 *sen* a serving, the equivalent
of 2,400 yen today (or about $22 at 2020 exchange rates).[27]

Another food writer, Shiraki Masamitsu, agreed with
Matsuzaki Tenmin's assessment that sushi places were at the
lower end of the restaurant spectrum, but Shiraki was a more
adventurous eater willing to try these dives and take his reader
with him. In *A Walker's Guide to Fine Food in the Greater Tokyo Area*
(*Dai Tōkyō umaimono tabearuki*), published in 1933, Shiraki wrote:

> Sushi places and soba shops are the quintessential plebeian
> eating places; nigiri costs one or two sen up to five sen. No
> matter how much one eats, one's pocketbook won't hurt
> much; but there are some vastly more expensive places out
> there, and one cannot be too careful when among the many
> food stands that appear to be crude. Most food stands will
> usually have their nigirizushi listed on a sign labelled accord-
> ing to the price, and one can do the sums in one's head and
> not make any mistakes.[28]

Shiraki identifies many low-end sushi places in Asakusa, a
part of Tokyo famous for its sushi and other vendors, as mentioned earlier. He counted fifteen sushi stands in Asakusa that
competed with eleven yakitori shops, ten establishments that
served beef on rice, ten that offered hotpot (*oden*), six ramen

shops, five tempura stands, three that sold Western dishes, and one that offered simmered foods. Many of these sushi stands were on Asakusa's informally named 'Sushi Side Street' (Sushi Yokocho).[29] One of these shops, Sennarizushi, was Shiraki's personal favourite:

> There are quite a few sushi stands where one stands and eats, but the owner here puts ice on top of the stand and piles the fish slices high on top to the point that one cannot see over them. There is a water spigot in front of the table for handwashing, and in the catch basin below gold fish swim brightly. The prices are reasonable here, but fresh ingredients are used.[30]

Some food stands found their fans even among discerning diners. Nagase Ganosuke, author of the 1930 book *Sushi Connoisseur* (*Sushi tsū*), cited popular wisdom to announce that the best sushi could only come from a food stand where one stood and ate. Sushi was, above all, a snack food; it did not constitute an entire meal, he explained.[31]

SUSHI'S DARK VALLEY: THE SECOND WORLD WAR

Despite their popularity, the central government prohibited stands selling sushi in 1939, contending that they were unsanitary.[32] That year all restaurants faced other restrictions under wartime mobilization and rationing. A December 1939 law prohibited the sale of white rice and mandated the use of brown rice. Polishing rice stripped off the healthy bran and reduced the size of the kernel, wasting food. To prevent entrepreneurs from polishing their own rice – something which could be easily done by pouring it into a large container such as a bottle and pounding it with a stick – in August 1940 restaurants in Tokyo were prevented from selling white rice, and they had to turn to rice substitutes such as finely cut buckwheat and wheat noodles. After 1941 dining out required a government-issued ticket, although some restaurants remained open in secret for customers who could afford them.[33] All remaining restaurants were ordered to close on 25 February 1944, but by that point in the war, food was hardly available in the major cities apart from on the black market.

Despite the many obvious negative effects of the war in ways too numerous to record here, some sushi historians find some positive developments. Japanese colonialism preceding and during the Second World War allegedly facilitated the spread of sushi. The Korean sushi roll called *gimbap*, a variation of makizushi that uses sesame oil instead of vinegar in the rice, is a culinary legacy of the colonial period (1910–45) in Korea, notwithstanding that the rice used to make it was also a symbol of Japanese colonial exploitation. The rice grown in Korea was exported to Japan, leaving the Korean population to make up the deficit with other grains imported from colonies or by doing without.[34] When the war turned against Japan, the bombing of Tokyo has been given as a reason for the dissemination of Tokyo-style sushi nationally as chefs fled the city and relocated to other parts of the country.[35]

The fact that nigirizushi is typically served in two pieces today is said to be another legacy of wartime deprivation, when different varieties of fish were scarce, causing chefs to serve two pieces of what they had on hand.[36] Serving two pieces of nigirizushi was also a way to disguise the fact that the sushi was smaller. It is probably during the Second World War and Occupation that nigirizushi assumed its current size, two-and-a-half times smaller than the sushi made at the beginning of the century. After the war, the smaller sizes allowed people to try a greater variety of toppings. The choice to serve two pieces of nigirizushi has also been explained as a way to differentiate the way sushi is served in restaurants from the religious practices of some families who placed a piece of sushi on the home altar as an offering to deceased relatives.[37] However, that theory does not explain why serving one piece of sushi was not considered to be a taboo before then.

FOLK SUSHI

Sushi restaurants suffered during the war, but people in rural areas continued to make sushi at home notwithstanding rationing, as one ethnographic survey launched just before the attack on Pearl Harbor in 1941 documented. The Imperial Rule Assistance Association, the equivalent of the Fascist Party in Japan, directed the Popular Traditions Association, a professional organization for folklorists known today as the Folklore Society of Japan, to conduct a survey of rural eating habits to understand how these might benefit the war effort. Unable to dispatch researchers to the countryside for fear they might be viewed as spies for asking questions in remote areas, the Popular Traditions Association reached out to its members living across the country and asked them to visit a nearby community and interview people there knowledgeable about local customs. The association supplied prospective interviewers with printed booklets containing a list of one hundred questions about local foodways. One of these questions, and its several sub-questions, enquired about sushi:

>Do you make sushi?
>What fish do you use?

Please explain how you prepare it and in what season.
Is there a certain day that sushi is eaten?[38]

The last question might relate to the length of time for
which the sushi was allowed to ferment, but it also spoke to the
concerns of folklorists of the Popular Traditions Association to
use food as a vehicle for understanding the rural psyche, which
they assumed would unlock a hitherto lost national culture. Not
every community reported making sushi. Of the 98 completed
surveys that survive from some 37 different locations, 57 reported on some local sushi. Despite difficulties with the survey's
methods, including the idiosyncratic ways the interviewers
recorded their data and selected their interviewees, the Popular
Traditions Association Survey offers a snapshot of the variety
of sushi made in rural areas throughout Japan in the first half
of the twentieth century.

At a time when nigirizushi had become synonymous
with sushi in Tokyo, only respondents from one community
in Aichi Prefecture indicated that they made this version of
sushi, although their response did not detail techniques and
ingredients.[39] However, thirteen communities reported that
they made inarizushi. Varieties of makizushi were even more
prevalent, with nineteen communities reporting creating them,
typically with simple ingredients. In a village in Yamanashi,
the recipe for makizushi called for rolling rice up with dried
gourd, lotus root, taro stalks, fish flakes (denbu), burdock, carrot
and fish sausage (chikuwa) to form rolls 3.5 cm (1½ in.) thick.
A community in Aichi used dried gourd, pickled daikon and
mustard greens for its makizushi.[40] Seven communities made
'five item' (gomoku) or 'scattered' sushi (chirashizushi), flavoured
rice mixed with small pieces of fish, mushrooms and pickled
vegetables.

WILDFLOWER CHIRASHIZUSHI

(2 servings)

Folk recipes for chirashizushi make use of the ingredients that are on hand or can be gathered. Most of the ingredients for this sushi recipe came from my garden. The bamboo, which proliferates like a weed, needs to be pulled out otherwise it will overrun everything. The shoots can be peeled and boiled for eating. In Kansas, bamboo shoots appear in mid-April, around the time that violets are in bloom and dandelions and wild onions begin to appear. The onions are pickled in this recipe: wash and remove the tops and roots of the onion bulbs; place the bulbs in a jar; then pour on a mixture of hot water, vinegar, and salt. Let that stand for a few hours, or until the onions take on a pickled taste.

Mulberry leaves, which also start appearing in April, have more protein than kale and inhibit glucose absorption. They can also be made into a wonderful tea, either in leaf form or processed like matcha.

When gathering wild plants, make sure that you choose an unpolluted area.

For the sushi rice:
2 cups (480 ml) cooked short-grain rice
1 tablespoon vinegar (rice or apple cider vinegar preferred)
2 teaspoons sugar
½ teaspoon salt
One handful each of:
bamboo shoots: boiled and chopped
pickled wild onion bulbs
mulberry leaves
boiled and chopped violets

dandelion flowers (with the stem removed)
3 oz (85 g) or one small package of smoked salmon (optional)

Mix a tablespoon of vinegar, the sugar and salt in a large bowl. Transfer the hot, cooked rice into the vinegar mixture. Mix it gently. Let it rest for 30 minutes to cool to room temperature.

Mix the wild onion bulbs, mulberry leaves and salmon into the rice, then decorate with the violets and dandelion flowers.

Wildflower chirashizushi with violets, dandelion and bamboo shoots.

Narezushi and namanare sushi-making also continued in some locales. A community in Shiga reported producing funazushi, as did another in Shizuoka, which made it only on special occasions. Rather than these fully fermented forms of narezushi, namanare sushi, with a shorter period of fermentation, were more prevalent. In Gunma Prefecture trout was fermented for twenty to thirty days in salt and rice. A hamlet in Niigata reported that until recently they had made sweetfish sushi, which they fermented with rice in barrels for fifteen days before the end of the year to be eaten as a celebratory New Year's dish. Shingle sushi (kokerazushi) was another medieval type of sushi that was still found in rural areas. The recipe for it in Gifu Prefecture called for salted or dried trout or salmon to be filleted and mixed with chopped carrot and konbu and placed in a pickling bucket with one-part kōji to ten parts rice. The sushi was eaten after the taste had turned sour.[41]

Sake and vinegar were among the additives used to hasten the fermentation of sushi, harkening back to the methods for making 'fast sushi' (hayazushi) that appeared in the early modern period. A village in Kagoshima made a pressed sushi with slices of sea bream, bamboo shoots, pickled daikon and Japanese pepper (sanshō) leaves placed with rice mixed with sake in a bucket and pressed with a heavy weight. So-called 'sake sushi' remains a local noted food for sale in Kagoshima today, where it is no longer usually made at home.[42] The leftover lees from sake-making (kasu) were employed to make cuttlefish and abalone sushi in Iwate Prefecture. However, most communities relied on vinegar as an additive for their sushi. A locale in Gifu made a mackerel sushi by removing the head and tail of a mackerel and salting it. The fish was then stuffed with rice flavoured with vinegar. Presumably after resting for some time, the fish was served whole, one for each person at special occasions. Serving

Sake sushi from Kagoshima.

an entire fish, usually sliced in pieces, was called 'whole sushi' (sugatazushi), which a community in Tokushima reported making with horse mackerel, sweetfish, mackerel and other fish that had been marinated in vinegar. As in Gifu, this was a dish reserved for special occasions.[43]

As these examples indicate, in rural Japan sushi was hardly a staple; instead, it was reserved for special events and holidays. A community in Mie Prefecture made sushi only for the autumn harvest festival. Aichi had its own harvest festival with sushi, but locals there sometimes made sushi as a packaged meal when travelling. In Niigata, sushi made with salted salmon was a food only for the New Year. In Tottori, the New Year called for a namanare sushi made from sweetfish, which was made as a sugatazushi with a mixture of rice and kōji packed into

the belly of the fish before allowing it to ferment in a pickling
barrel. Local residents were fond of it, but outsiders apparently
avoided it. Weddings, local festivals and seasonal observations
such as Girls' Day on 3 March were other occasions when sushi
was served in rural Japan.[44]

Equally telling are the explanations of when sushi was not
made. In some instances, the interviewers failed to record an
answer for the questions about sushi, but at other times they
reported that the community did not eat or make any sushi.
The community of Tsubune in Niigata did not make fermented
sushi because local legend said that the nearby deities did not
like it. However, that taboo did not prevent locals from making
makizushi, inarizushi and gomokuzushi, so it was probably the
fermented varieties of sushi that the deities were believed to
dislike. Other respondents in Niigata and Kagoshima stated
that they did not have access to fish, so could not make sushi,
while villagers in Tokyo Prefecture indicated that they bought
their sushi from restaurants. In communities in Fukushima and
Nagano, no one had ever heard of sushi, and one respondent
in Fukushima recalled that he might have tried inarizushi at a
festival once when he was a child.[45]

While a lack of fish prevented some communities from
making sushi, others relied on vegetarian ingredients and
canned seafood. Residents in a village in Nagano explained, 'We
make sushi but only rarely do we use fish.' Instead they made
norimaki, stuffed, presumably, with pickles or vegetables, and
inarizushi. The survey documented a famous local sushi from
Akita Prefecture usually made with sandfish (*hatahata*) combined
with slices of turnips and carrots, called *hatahatazushi*, but in this
case it was created instead with salmon and shrimp. In Ishikawa,
dried trout was used with daikon for sushi, which caused the
surveyor to reflect that the reason for this was because the locals

Hatahatazushi.

rarely had fresh fish. For sushi, the same community used salted fish and *tsukudani*, fish preserved by being boiled in a mixture of soy sauce, sugar and mirin until the liquid evaporates. Residents in Kyoto used canned mackerel or salmon for sushi and only rarely had access to fresh fish.[46]

Up until and during the Second World War, communities 30–50 km (20–30 mi.) from the coast had difficulty obtaining fish that was not salted or dried, and fresh seafood was often not available outside coastal fishing villages.[47] The lack of fresh fish helps to explain why the popularization of nigirizushi had to wait until the spread of refrigeration in the post-war era. Commercial refrigerators for the home became more widely available in the 1960s, but even by 1970, only 83 per cent of rural homes had a refrigerator.[48]

The advent of refrigeration and other post-war changes in the diet meant that traditional methods of sushi-making as a means of preserving fish were no longer a necessity. While some forms of rural sushi disappeared in the 1960s, others were rediscovered as 'local cuisine', laying the groundwork for a movement to preserve and commodify local food culture that first emerged in the late 1960s, but really took off in the 1980s and has continued to this day.[49] A 2015 Internet survey of 1,000 people nationally aged 20–59 indicated that 36.7 per cent had tried a 'local sushi', specifically trout sushi from Toyama Prefecture, in which trout that have been marinated in vinegar are placed on top of sushi rice and wrapped up in bamboo leaves.[50] However, other types of regional sushi were not as well sampled. Only 11.5 per cent of those surveyed had tried *tekone sushi* (a type of kokerazushi) from Mie Prefecture, 5.9 per cent had sampled funazushi from Shiga, and just 0.8 per cent had eaten sake sushi from Kagoshima, one of the varieties documented in the

Tekone sushi.

aforementioned study by folklorists. More telling is the fact that
37.6 per cent of respondents had never tried any of these forms
of local sushi, indicating that regional types of sushi remain
little more than a curiosity for most sushi eaters in Japan.[51]

SUSHI AFTER THE WAR

Food stands made a resurgence in Tokyo after the war in the various black markets that cropped up there. One black market in
Shinjuku appeared just five days after Japan's surrender, followed
by others in the city's main transportation hubs of Shibuya,
Shinbashi, Yūrakuchō, Kanda, Ueno and Ikebukuro. The stands,
many of which were operated by former soldiers and Korean
residents, sold a variety of goods and daily necessities, but were
most noted for their bootleg liquor. In 1947 some three hundred
drinking establishments operated in Yūrakuchō.[52] Other vendors
sold foods. Yakitori shops, ostensibly offering chicken, sold
less desirable cuts of meat such as pork intestines, heart, liver
and cartilage all cooked on a stick.[53] And ramen, made with U.S.
wheat, became a favourite food of black-market visitors seeking
a fatty, filling yet inexpensive meal.

However, sushi faced a more difficult time making a comeback. Pre-war laws against sushi stands continued after the
war, and rice was in scarce supply to the point that restaurants,
excepting those that catered to Allied troops, were prohibited
from operating until 1949. In response, the Tokyo Prefecture
Sushi Business Association successfully lobbied the prefectural
government for the right to serve customers who brought their
own rice. The traditional measurement of one gō (180 ml, ¾ cup)
of rice allowed customers to purchase ten pieces of nigirizushi
or makizushi. Sushi chefs could only use freshwater fish or
shellfish, since other seafood was still restricted. Customers

could also barter with other ingredients such as eggs, shiitake or dried gourd, which sushi chefs needed. Sushi associations in other prefectures followed suit, and this facilitated the spread of the custom of eating nigirizushi. The ruling also helped make the ten-piece order of sushi standard.[54]

With the post-war economic recovery, sushi restaurants could afford to install refrigeration, which allowed chefs to keep a greater variety of fish on hand where previously they had had to work with smaller fish or fish that could be quickly consumed. Sushi chefs could thereby add sea bream and other white-flesh fish to expand their repertoire. Fatty tuna (toro) be-came a delicacy in Japan from the 1960s thanks to refrigeration technology and consumers' changing preference for fatty foods.[55] Japan's share in the global consumption of tuna, which includes bluefin and skipjack (katsuo), climbed more than 40 per cent in the second half of the twentieth century, fifteen times Japan's share of the world population growth in the same period.[56]

JAPAN'S LOCAL CUISINES

The cookbook *Japan's Local Cuisines* (Nihon no kyōdo ryōri), published first in 1966 and then in a revised version in 1974, capitalized on the growing nostalgia for rural life by promising readers that it delivered cuisine from the hometowns of each of Japan's 47 prefectures.[57] The book contains a number of sushi recipes including ones for a stuffed squid sushi from Aomori Prefecture. The length of time for which the sushi is allowed to ferment is unspecified, notwithstanding the author's comment that the luxury of having reliable indoor heating has hastened the fermentation process considerably.

SQUID SUSHI

Ingredients (to make servings for four people):
2 squid; 3 cups [720 ml] sushi rice; ¼ carrot;
3 tablespoons green peas.

Preparation:
1) Remove the tentacles from the squid and the skin, then wash carefully and briefly boil. Cover with vinegar and allow to marinate.
2) Boil the carrot and cut into 5 mm [¼ in.] segments and mix with the green peas [and rice]. Stuff the squid with this.
3) Place the squid in a pickling bucket with a heavy weight stone on top, so it can be eaten in midwinter. These days, thanks to modern indoor heating, the dish can be served soon after it is made. The squid tentacles can be boiled, finely chopped and also added to the rice.

The same text also provides a recipe for salmon sushi from Fukushima Prefecture that uses kōji powder to facilitate fermentation.

SALMON SUSHI

Ingredients (to make servings for four people):
1 kg [2 lb 3 oz] salmon; 100 g [3½ oz] salt;
480 ml [2 cups] glutinous rice; kōji

Preparation:
1) Clean the salmon and salt the large pieces as if making salted salmon.
2) Place the glutinous rice in a pot. Slice the salmon into large chunks and arrange them in the pot. Sprinkle on the salt and kōji and add layers of salmon, rice, salt, and kōji until the pot is full. Sprinkle the remaining salt and kōji on the top and put on the floating lid with a heavy weight on top of it. Let rest for around three days.
3) Remove any water that emerges over the top of the lid. When it seems that no more water will come out, the fish can be sliced and eaten.[58]

THE PROFESSIONALIZATION OF SUSHI CHEFS

It was theoretically possible for anyone to open a sushi stand before the Second World War, but in the post-war period the government asserted more control over the qualifications for becoming a sushi chef. As a result, sushi education became more formalized. While some sushi chefs may have taught themselves the trade, others seeking more rigorous training entered the profession through a traditional apprenticeship system that lasted approximately ten to fifteen years or more and started in adolescence for boys.

In the sushi world, trainees traditionally spend three years as a fledgling, five years as a helper and seven to ten years as a journeyman. That means that in the first three years, an apprentice washes dishes, makes tea and helps prep ingredients while gradually learning how to cut fish and make makizushi. After three to five years, apprentices can be trusted to cut fish on their own. Journeymen are high enough status that they can substitute for the boss on his day off, and focus on learning how to run a successful sushi business. After this process, with their skills and their own capital or loans, the sushi trainees are supposed to be qualified enough to be able to open their own establishments.[59]

After the war, this informal apprentice system became more formalized. In 1958 the government began issuing licences, which required passing an exam to qualify as a chef (chōrishi). In 1983 the government introduced a specialized sushi chef licence, which required taking an exam administered by the local prefectural government or the national government. In practice, however, such a licence is not needed to open a sushi restaurant. All one needs is permission from the prefectural department of health. Anyone can prepare sushi in a restaurant without a licence; however, they cannot legally refer to them-selves as a sushi chef without one.[60] Licences do bring more prestige. In 2018 Ogawa Hirotoshi recalled that when he entered the trade 25 years ago, many of the senior workers at the sushi restaurant came from dubious backgrounds, but today the image of the sushi chef has improved to the point that some appear on television and the trade no longer has a negative image.[61]

In the patriarchal world of the traditional culinary arts, until recently female sushi chefs were a rarity in Japan. Chef Ogawa explained that it was the traditional family structure of the Japanese household and the long hours working that kept women in the home to raise children, rather than the errone-ous notions that women could not become sushi chefs because they menstruated or because they had warmer hands than men. However, in recent years the numbers of women sushi chefs have been increasing.[62] Moreover, even though women may not be formally recognized as sushi chefs, many small sushi restau-rants are operated by couples who divide the work between them, and this has been a long-standing pattern.[63]

CONVEYOR-BELT SUSHI

Sushi is no longer sold at outdoor food stands, but serving the market for inexpensive sushi restaurants are conveyor-belt (*kaiten*) sushi places where anyone can sit down alone or with friends and select from the sushi that passes by, based upon what appeals to them and according to the price, as indicated by the different colours of plates used. The invention of conveyor-belt sushi is credited to Shiraishi Yoshiaki (1914–2001), the owner of the sushi shop Genroku in Osaka. Genroku opened in 1950, and inspired by a visit to a meat-packing factory (or, according to other versions of the story, a beer-bottling plant), the owner of Genroku experimented with installing a conveyor belt in his business in 1958. Customers could readily understand the cost of each serving of sushi by looking at the colour of the plate it was on, which was another advantage over higher-end sushi bars, which did not usually list prices. Following pre-war traditions and perhaps in a further effort to economize, customers initially had to stand at Shiraishi's sushi restaurant, but eventually he added bar stools.[64]

Shiraishi's idea took off, enabling him to open 250 branch restaurants, including a temporary one at the Osaka International Expo in 1970. That event was a watershed moment for the restaurant trade in Japan, helping to usher in a new wave of dining out among families and young people. In 1974 Kita Nihon Kakō Corporation introduced a conveyor-belt sushi bar with hot water spigots, allowing customers to make their own tea using cups and tea bags. The owners of conveyor-belt sushi places could order

Conveyor-belt sushi restaurant, Kagoshima, 2009.

pre-sliced and processed fish, which allowed them to de-skill and speed up the production process, facilitating the growth of these sushi establishments in the 1970s and '80s.[65] The same company introduced a machine in 1980 that made nigirizushi, creating 'sushi made by robots'. And two major conveyor-belt sushi chains launched in that year, Atom Boy Sushi and Genki Sushi. Genki Sushi now has overseas branches in Taiwan, China, Kuwait and the United States.[66] By one estimate, in 2008 there were some 5,000 to 6,000 conveyor-belt sushi places in Japan alone.[67] Conveyor-belt sushi places made sushi inexpensive enough to be not only a snack but a meal as well.

A 2015 Internet survey of 1,000 Japanese people about their dining habits at conveyor-belt sushi restaurants found that 81.9 per cent ate at them, and of those, 25 per cent of men and 21.5 per cent of women went there monthly. Beyond conveyor-belt sushi restaurants, the same survey revealed that 66.2 per cent of respondents also purchased takeaway sushi from places such as supermarkets. Only 27.2 per cent reported making any sushi at home.[68] With the greater availability of inexpensive sushi, whether from a conveyor-belt sushi restaurant or a takeaway store, sushi is no longer a delicacy for special occasions; instead, it has become a daily convenience food, according to sushi chef Ogawa Hirotoshi.[69]

One of the major takeaway sushi businesses was Kozō Sushi, which sold its products both to supermarkets and in its own establishments. Kozō's founder, Yamaki Masuji (b. 1936), was born into the sushi business. When he was a child, his father's restaurant used the room where he slept as a dining area, forcing him to do his homework at a teacher's house. After putting himself through college, Yamaki returned to the family business, marrying and opening his own sushi restaurant in Tenkajaya Osaka in 1962. Yamaki's father had once operated a sushi stand, and Yamaki thought there would be an opportunity to do something similar by opening a small shop for takeaway sushi in a shopping arcade in 1964. On the opening day he made six hundred large makizushi (*futomakizushi*) and sold them all in three hours. Local supermarkets began carrying his products too, and he opened more takeaway stands, eventually offering franchises of his business in 1972 following the model of American fast-food restaurant chains. By 1987 there were 2,300 stores in the Kozō Sushi chain.[70] As of June 2020 that number has fallen to 201 outlets, 125 of which were franchises. The company also runs a chain of ramen shops and another of takeaway sushi places called Chagetsu, with fourteen stores.[71] Kozō Sushi's decline, as measured in the drop in the number of its outlets, was not caused by a falloff in demand for sushi, but from competition from conveyor-belt sushi places, which also started offering takeaway, and other sushi shops that used home delivery services such as Uber Eats.[72]

Today sushi, particularly nigirizushi, is a food that is eaten outside of the home, and it is no longer solely a snack food but more often a full meal. The same Internet survey cited above found that 52 per cent of men eat between ten and fourteen plates of sushi on a visit to a conveyor-belt sushi restaurant, while 45.8 per cent of women eat six to nine plates. Since each plate holds two pieces of nigirizushi (or between four and six pieces of makizushi), that translates into 20 to 28 pieces of nigirizushi for men and twelve to eighteen for women, in both cases a higher amount than the post-war serving of ten pieces. And there are those who truly gorge themselves: 15.2 per cent of men admitted to eating 15 to 29 plates, as did 2.8 per cent of women. In fact, these numbers might be even higher, considering that some sushi diners may have under-reported what they consumed.[73]

Large sushi roll (futomakizushi), Katori City, Chiba, 2009.

The growth in conveyor-belt sushi stores and takeaway operations coincided with the post-war steady increase in fish consumption in Japan. This was made possible by the 'economic miracle', marked by an average annual GDP growth rate of 10 per cent from 1950 to 1973. From 1950 to 2000 Japanese seafood consumption increased by 50 per cent. During that period, Japan grew to become the world's largest importer of seafood, feeding the highest per capita seafood supply worldwide, some 75 kg (165 lb) per capita in 2008 compared with 20 kg (44 lb) for the U.S. and Britain and 30 kg (66 lb) for France. That translates into about 150 g (5.3 oz) of seafood per person per day in Japan, once non-human uses for fish such as for animal feed are subtracted. As much as the world has come to love sushi, and the Japanese government has worked hard to promote a 'traditional' fish-based diet within Japan and abroad, Vaclav Smil and Kazuhiko

Kobayashi point out in their longitudinal study of the Japanese diet that global fish stocks, which are already overharvested, would disappear were the rest of the world to follow Japan's love of seafood.[74]

Conveyor-belt sushi places, along with the sushi available in supermarkets and convenience stories, represent the lower end of the food trade in terms of pricing and quality, but high-end sushi restaurants are equally visible, albeit fewer in number. Chief among these today is the famous Sukiyabashi Jirō in Tokyo, made famous in the 2011 documentary *Jiro Dreams of Sushi*. It was the first sushi restaurant to receive three Michelin stars, which it held from its first listing in 2007 to 2019, when Jirō was de-listed because it no longer accepts reservations from the general public. Sukiyabashi Jirō is where Prime Minister Abe

The Sushi Summit: President Barack Obama meets sushi master Ono Jirō, owner of Sukiyabashi Jirō sushi restaurant, during a private dinner with Prime Minister Abe Shinzō of Japan in Tokyo, 23 April 2014.

invited President Barack Obama to dine in April 2014, a meal that one reporter dubbed the 'sushi summit'.[75] But in Tokyo, a city which has more Michelin-starred restaurants than anywhere else in the world, one can find 36 other sushi restaurants with listings in the 2020 *Michelin Guide Tokyo*, if one can afford them.[76] A meal at Sukiyabashi Jirō starts at 40,000 yen ($372 at 2020 exchange rates) per person.[77] Tokyo's quintessential street food has certainly come a long way.

FIVE
THE GLOBAL SPREAD OF SUSHI

Today, sushi is a global food, both in how it is consumed and how it is sourced. According to Japan's Ministry of Agriculture, Forestry and Fisheries (MAFF), as of 2017, there were some 117,500 Japanese restaurants globally, up from 89,000 in 2015 and 24,000 in 2006. Most of these (69,300) were in Asia outside Japan, which as of 2016 had 20,135 sushi shops.[1] By region, North America has 25,300 Japanese restaurants, Western Europe 12,200 and South America 4,600; Russia and Australia each have 2,400, and there are 950 Japanese restaurants in the Middle East and 350 in Africa.[2] Japanese restaurants have existed in China since before the fall of the Qing dynasty (1644–1912), and the first Japanese-owned restaurant in America dates to 1885.[3]

When Japan opened more freely for international trade after the mid-nineteenth century, travellers to Japan encountered sushi, along with other Japanese foods, but the global sushi boom occurred after the Second World War, beginning in the United States in the late 1960s and spreading internationally in the 1980s and '90s. Initially, non-Japanese had to have sushi defined for them. A short article that ran in the *Los Angeles Times* in 1957 told travellers to Japan to expect something called sushi on their flight: 'Northwest Orient Airlines advises tourists that sushi is a rice sandwich that is popular with natives and visitors.'[4] As sushi spread, it evolved in meaning outside Japan from a food once deemed unpalatable – if not dangerous – to one that was chic, healthy and now popular to the point of being mundane.

However, the global spread of sushi has increased demands on fish populations. Fish do not respect state boundaries, and they are unevenly protected by international laws. Restrictions can be placed on bluefin tuna at one side of the Atlantic while the worst industrial fishing practices are allowed to continue on the other.[5]

The degree to which sushi is healthy or dangerous has also become a point of global debate. When the Fukushima nuclear disaster occurred in March 2011, observers on the other side of the Pacific wondered if their sushi was safe to eat. This chapter examines the global spread of sushi, from restaurants, to fishing, to international health concerns related to fishing and to sushi consumption. However, the fate of conveyor-belt sushi operations around the world in the wake of the spread of the novel coronavirus (Covid-19) remains uncertain at the time of the writing of this book.

SUSHI COMES TO AMERICA

Charles Kame (also known as Hamada Hamanojo) opened the first Japanese-owned restaurant in North America in Los Angeles in 1885.[6] The Kame Restaurant, located on East First Street in an area of the city that would come to be known as Little Tokyo, served Western food, as did two other Japanese-owned restaurants that operated near the Little Tokyo area by 1892. The first Japanese-owned restaurant to serve Japanese food opened in San Francisco in 1887; it was called the Yamato. Six years later, greater Los Angeles had its first restaurant that served Japanese food, the Mihatei, which opened next to a public bath in Chinatown in 1893. It was followed by several others in that section of the city.[7]

There are some claims that sushi was served in a restaurant in Little Tokyo as early as 1906, but the quintessential Japanese restaurant food in the United States (for white people at least) through to the 1960s was sukiyaki, beef cooked in a pot with vegetables.[8] One guidebook to Japanese food published in 1946 dubbed sukiyaki 'the national dish of Japan similar to roast beef of England', while at the same time warning non-Japanese readers away from dishes such as sashimi and sushi that would 'repel and disgust them'.[9] Japanese restaurateurs also operated Chinese 'chop suey' restaurants, and there were as many as sixty of these Japanese-owned businesses in Los Angeles by 1927, serving inexpensive fare to a Caucasian clientele.[10]

Despite the Gentlemen's Agreement of 1907 prohibiting adult male Japanese from emigrating to the United States, according to one report, by 1909 there were 149 Japanese-owned restaurants in the Western United States that served American food, and 232 more that specialized in Japanese cooking. The 1915 Los Angeles telephone directory, among other records, shows 715 Japanese-owned businesses that included Western and Japanese restaurants, miso manufacturers, sake brewers, rice sellers, vegetable stands and butcher's shops, making it possible to buy locally produced fishcake (kamaboko), Japanese noodles, nattō, senbei and soy sauce in Los Angeles.[11] The initial burst in energy was derailed by the 1924 Immigration Act, which ended all Asian emigration to the u.s., including Japanese. The Second World War not only brought the closure of Japanese restaurants on the West Coast, but saw the forced removal and internment of U.S. citizens of Japanese descent from California and other states in 1942.

One Little Tokyo restaurant that survived the war may have also been the first to sell sushi to Japanese and white customers. Japanese émigré Kawasaki Yasujirō (1892–1978) opened Matsunosushi (also Matsu no Sushi) on 111 San Pedro Street in 1921. A reporter for the *Shin Sekai*, a Japanese newspaper in San Francisco, described the fare, mentioning the sushi in passing and commenting on the inexpensively priced rice bowls (*donburi*) costing 25 cents that drew white college students.[12] In 1933 Kawasaki moved his restaurant to 313 East First Street. An announcement in the Los Angeles Japanese newspaper the *Rafu Shimpo* stated that the new venue would 'cater to the Japanese and a few American sushi-eaters'.[13] Kawasaki registered the new building in the names of his children, since foreign-born Japanese could not own property.[14] In 1937 photographer Herman Schultheis captured an image of a white man peering into the art deco window of Matsunosushi. A writer for the *Rafu Shimpo* advised that the owner of the establishment label the nigirizushi visible to customers through the window:

> If I were to single out a distinctively artistic window in all Li'l Tokio, I would not hesitate in naming that of the Matsu no Sushi. It is on East First near San Pedro. I have seen from time to time American passers-by pausing in front of that window to see and admire the exotic beauties displayed by it. I only wish that they added in a harmonious way a 'foot-note' in English explaining what it is all about. SUSHI – 'Japanese sandwiches' – 25 cents. Or something like that.
>
> It also makes me think how wonderful it might be if passers-by could stand in front of the window and see how Sushi are actually made.[15]

Herman J. Schultheis, photograph of Matsunosushi
Restaurant, 1937.

Matsunosushi reopened in 1947 and the store operated until the
death of Yasujirō in 1978, when mention of the establishment
disappeared from the *Rafu Shimpo*.

After the Second World War, only 56 restaurants owned
by Japanese remained in Los Angeles in 1954. Of these, sixteen
served Japanese food, nine sold Chinese and 31 were Western-
style eateries.[16] New York's three Japanese restaurants, one of
which, the Miyako, opened in 1910, were also closed because of
the Second World War.[17] Legal immigration from Japan did not

resume until the passing of the Immigration Act of 1965, which lifted the ban on Japanese as well as other Asians and Southern and Eastern Europeans from becoming U.S. citizens.

In the post-war heyday of sukiyaki in the United States, Honolulu was the only locale where sushi could be found regularly in restaurants in the early to mid-1950s. *Japanese Foods (Tested Recipes)*, a cookbook published in 1956 by the Hui Manaolana, a Japanese residents' organization in Honolulu, not only contained recipes for nigirizushi and makizushi, but displayed advertisements for several restaurants selling sushi. The Wisteria Restaurant at the corner of King and Piikoi Streets announced 'Tokyo Sushi' as its speciality and also offered 'excellent American Style food'. Another restaurant located on 1309 Kalakaua Avenue billed itself as a 'Sushi Center' and claimed its speciality was sushi. Finally, Tsujita Tempura on Beretania Street sold takeaway sushi.[18]

The 1960s saw the first hints that sushi was catching on in the mainland United States, according to American newspapers. Noted food critic Craig Claiborne (1920–2000) observed in 1963 that sushi was too 'far out' for some New York diners, who preferred teriyaki. Three years later, in a column of restaurant reviews, Claiborne described the dramatic proliferation of Japanese restaurants in Manhattan and his characterization of sushi had changed completely. Claiborne identified Kamehachi as a sushi restaurant located on 41 West 46th Street and the older, 'grande luxe' Nippon on 145 East 52nd Street, which had its own sushi bar and served the best 'raw fish and vinegared rice' anywhere in the city. New Yorkers 'for whom "Chopsticks" was once a childish piano exercise' had not only become accustomed to Japanese food, but 'some of them dine on the raw fish dishes, sushi and sashimi, with a gusto once reserved for corn flakes.'[19] The Nippon opened in 1963, two years after New York's

JAPANESE FOODS (TESTED RECIPES)

The cookbook *Japanese Foods (Tested Recipes)*, published in 1956 by the Hui Manaolana, a Japanese residents' organization in Honolulu, contains directions for making sushi rice and six different recipes for sushi. For sushi rice, the authors suggest boiling the rice with konbu for the first three minutes of cooking time, a typical technique to make the rice savoury thanks to the naturally occurring MSG in the konbu. Further flavouring of the rice comes from the addition of a mixture of ⅓ cup (80 ml) vinegar, five tablespoons of sugar, one tablespoon of salt and two teaspoons of 'gourmet powder'. The powder is artificial MSG, specified as the Japanese product Ajinomoto, used in many of the recipes and featured in a full-page advertisement in the cookbook. The ingredients are heated in a saucepan until the sugar and salt dissolve, then added to the hot rice, which is cooled by fanning it with a fan.

The recipe for Maguro Nigiri Sushi, credited to Mrs Tooka Ida, relies on the sushi rice recipe. It also uses tuna (called *shibi* in both Hawai'i and in Japan) and mustard or horseradish instead of wasabi.

MAGURO NIGIRI SUSHI

Servings: 6–8
1½ lb shibi (tuna)
1 teaspoon mustard paste or grated horseradish
Prepare 4 cups rice for sushi.

While the rice is cooling, cut fish into slices 1½" × 2" × ⅛" [4 cm × 5 cm × 3 mm], a little larger than for sashimi. Make small rice balls shaped like an egg, slightly flattened, and press a slice of shibi on top. Dab a little mustard or horseradish between the rice and fish.

Brush taré sauce on the fish with pastry brush.

Taré sauce:

¾ cup shoyu [soy sauce], 1 tablespoon sake, 1 teaspoon sugar. Cook over slow [*sic*] heat until thickened.

Variations:

Use boiled shrimp opened flat and soaked in vinegar.[20]

first post-war Japanese restaurant Kabuki. Kitcho, a branch of the famous restaurant by the same name in Kyoto, debuted in 1964, the same year Benihana opened in New York. Like Benihana, Kamehachi, which opened in 1965 in New York City, was one of a chain of fifteen Japanese restaurants in the USA.[21] Kamehachi also opened a branch in Chicago in 1967 operated by nisei Marion Konishi, niece of the restaurant's founder.[22] It was originally located on 1617 North Wells Street across the street from Chicago's famous improvisation theatre The Second City, and actor John Belushi was said to have become a regular customer at Kamehachi. In the 1970s he would frequently appear on *Saturday Night Live* as a samurai in different occupations, including as a chef.[23]

Sushi restaurants were starting to open in California in the same period in the 1960s, most of which were operated by second-generation Japanese owners without professional training as chefs. In Los Angeles' Little Tokyo's Kawafuku restaurant was the first place to have a sushi counter with a glass case in 1965 (or 1962, according to some scholars).[24] It was joined by two other sushi shops in the 1960s, although other eateries sold sushi too.

— MENU —

DINNER—3:00 PM to 10:00 PM

Choice of MISO SHIRU (soya bean soup) or SUIMONO (clear soup)
RICE - PICKLES - TEA and DESSERT with all DINNERS

For something new and different, try SUSHI for appetizer! 1.00

1. **TEI SHOKU DINNER** (Table D'Hote) 1.70
   Complete Japanese dinner
2. **SASHIMI DINNER** 1.25
   Fillet of fresh raw fish and shitashi (boiled spinach)
3. **TEMPURA DINNER** 1.25
   Fried butterfly shrimps and sunomono (salad)
4. **YAKI TORI DINNER** 1.60
   Chicken broiled in tare sauce and fresh vegetable salad
5. **YAKI BUTA DINNER** 1.60
   Pork broiled in tare sauce and fresh vegetable salad
6. **YAKI NIKU DINNER** 1.75
   Beef broiled in tare sauce and fresh vegetable salad
7. **UNAGI DINNER** 1.60
   Eels broiled in tare sauce and sunomono (salad)

Our Specialty

SUKIYAKI DINNER #1 .... 1.75
(Beef, pork or chicken)
SUKIYAKI DINNER #2 .... 1.95
(Beef, pork or chicken) & Tempura (fried butterfly shrimps)
SUKIYAKI DINNER #3 .... 2.20
Tempura (fried butterfly shrimps) & Sunomono (sea food salad)

8. **SUSHI DINNER** 1.25
   Vinegared rice ovals with shrimp; squid; clam and sea weed roll
9. **TEN DON DINNER** 1.20
   Fried butterfly shrimps on rice in large covered bowl.
10. **KATSU DONBURI DINNER** 1.20
    Pork cutlets and egg on rice in large covered bowl
11. **OYAKO DONBURI DINNER** 1.20
    Chicken and egg on rice in large covered bowl
12. **UNAGI DONBURI DINNER** 1.45
    Broiled eels on rice in large covered bowl

MINIMUM — $1.00 PER PERSON

A LA CARTE

SUIMONO OR MISO SHIRU (clear soup or soya bean soup)	.20
SASHIMI (fillet of fresh raw fish)	.60
SUNOMONO (assorted sea food salad, Japanese style)	.60
TERI-YAKI (broiled fish in sauce)	.55
SHITASHI (boiled spinach)	.35
YAKI-NORI (toasted sea weed)	.35
GOMA-AYE (boiled spinach in crushed sesame sauce)	.40
NUTA (boiled scallion and sea food with special soya bean sauce)	.60
YAKI-TAMAGO (fried eggs, Japanese style)	.55
YU-DOFU (hot soya bean curd)	.50
YAKKO-DOFU (cold soya bean curd)	.35
TEMPURA (fried butterfly shrimps)	.75
SUSHI (vinegared rice ovals with shrimp, squid, clam and sea weed roll)	1.00
SUSHI (To take out, boxed)	1.35
GOHAN (rice)	.15
TSUKEMONO (pickles)	.25
YAKI NIKU (beef broiled in tare sauce)	1.35
YAKI BUTA (pork broiled in tare sauce)	1.35
YAKI TORI (chicken broiled in tare sauce)	1.40
SUKIYAKI (beef pork or chicken)	1.55
ICE CREAM	.30
FRUITS IN SEASON	.25

DONBURI A LA CARTE

YOSE-NABE (large portion) (chicken, fish and mixed vegetables soup) Served with rice.	1.70
OKAME UDON (mixed Japanese vegetables on noodles)	.75
OYAKO UDON (chicken and egg on noodles)	.65
TEMPURA UDON (fried butterfly shrimps on noodles)	.65
TSUKIMI UDON (raw egg on noodles)	.55
SU UDON (plain sauce on noodles)	.45
HIYASHI SOMEN (cold thin noodles on ice with sauce)	.55
ZARU SOBA (cold wheat noodles with sauce)	.60
OYAKO DONBURI (chicken and egg on rice)	.95
TEN DON (fried butterfly shrimps on rice)	.95
KATSU DONBURI (pork cutlets and egg on rice)	.95
UNAGI DONBURI (broiled eels on rice)	1.20

WINE — BEER — SOFT DRINKS

JAPANESE SAKE (imported)	Bottle	1.00
JAPANESE SAKE (Hawaiian)	Bottle	.85
KIRIN BEER		.65
SCHLITZ		.35
BUDWEISER		.35
FABST BLUE RIBBON		.35
PORT		.40
SHERRY		.40
SAUTERNE		.40
BURGUNDY		.40
COCA COLA		.15
SEVEN UP		.15

Menu cover and interior from Tsuruya Restaurant, 1957, based at 239 West 105th Street in New York.

Until 1970 most of Los Angeles's Japanese restaurants were in Little Tokyo, but that began to change as restaurateurs opened establishments in other neighbourhoods and the number of Japanese restaurants went from 34 in 1969 to 148 by 1979.[25] The dominant explanation for the initial growth of Japanese restaurants in the United States in the 1960s is that they were built to cater to Japanese businessmen and their families working and living abroad. However, the proliferation of Japanese restaurants in the 1970s was thanks to the fact that they had found a larger market.

Matsumoto Hirotaka, a Japanese restaurateur who began work in the trade in New York in 1970, offered several reasons why sushi began to catch on in the U.S. with non-Japanese diners. He observed that initially the only non-Japanese who ventured into Japanese restaurants were people who had lived and travelled in Japan or were 'hippies', part of the 1960s counter-culture. However, the influx of Japanese consumer goods from the 1970s and increased interaction with Japanese living in the United States introduced Americans to Japanese food, but it took time for Americans to shift their preferences from sukiyaki to sushi. According to Matsumoto, most Americans thought all fish tasted the same because they cooked them all the same way, either in butter or by frying. Sushi, in contrast, provided a way to understand how different varieties of fish tasted. Americans also liked the performance aspects of sushi prepared in front of them at a sushi bar, where people could sample a little sushi without having to order a full meal, in contrast to a French restaurant, where one could never dine alone lest one be seated near the bathroom. A final reason Matsumoto and many others cite for the popularity of sushi was that it came to be considered a health food after the United States Senate Select Committee on Nutrition and Human Needs published the McGovern

Report in 1977. Named for the committee's chairman, Senator George McGovern, the report suggested that Americans shift away from fatty and processed foods. In contrast to beef, sushi was a health food.[26]

Sushi was presented in the American press as both the representative food of Japan and the country's most exotic and elevated culinary achievement, which further enhanced its status. Reporters followed the lead of Craig Claiborne, who wrote in 1968, 'although it has never been declared as such, the dish called sushi may be the national dish of Japan.' Claiborne made this declaration even as he had to define sushi for his readers: 'sushi is, of course, an assortment of small morsels of the freshest raw fish and sea food pressed onto cold rice lightly seasoned with vinegar.'[27] Seven years later, Claiborne was still introducing sushi to apprehensive readers, hinting that those who had yet to try it were somehow lacking in their understanding of cuisine. He wrote in 1975 in a column carried both in the *New York Times* and the *Chicago Tribune*, 'to the uninitiated palate, sushi – raw fish served on rice – is one of the gastronomic curiosities of the world . . . To those who enjoy sushi, however, it is one of the gastronomic wonders, in or out of its native Japan.'[28] The year before Claiborne wrote that article, there were more than 150 Japanese restaurants in New York City.[29]

The claim that sushi was the 'national dish of Japan' was significant in light of Japan's growing economic presence in the 1970s. Japan may have ended its double-digit growth rate in the 1970s and suffered a brief recession in 1974, but Japanese exports to the United States increased steadily to the point that by the mid-1980s, they were double American exports to Japan. Prompted by lobbyists from industries and labour unions, the U.S. negotiated limits on Japanese exports in the 1970s, including steel, colour televisions and cars, in 1981.[30] At the same time

American consumers were turning to Japanese goods, they also embraced Japanese food. 'Part of the strength of Japanese cuisine in American restaurants', writes food scholar Krishnendu Ray, 'is related to the rise of Japan as a major economic and cultural power which has made its food an exotic "foreign" commodity, a designer commodity if you will, somewhat akin to the role once played by French food in the American imagination'.[31] Reporter Barry Hillenbrand titled his 1980 article about sushi for the *Chicago Tribune* 'From the Folks Who Brought You Sony Comes a Fishy Ritual in the Raw'. Hillenbrand equated the rise of sushi to the greater economic power of Japan, writing:

> As platoons of white-shirted Japanese businessmen have
> gone abroad to make the world safe for Japan, Inc., they have
> established what amounts to field kitchens serving *sushi* in
> Los Angeles, New York, and to a limited extent, Chicago.[32]

Sushi may have been described as a Japanese national dish in American newspapers, but food writers in the 1970s explained that Americans needed initiation into how to eat it. Jane Salzfass Freiman, writing for the *Chicago Tribune*, described sushi as 'Japan's fast food', but one that required specific cultural knowledge for Americans to order. Not only do sushi chefs 'have barely a nodding acquaintance with the English language', she expounded, 'mastering the art of ordering and eating sushi is a delightful introduction to the complex cuisine of Japan and a fascinating odyssey through a strange and totally Japanese world of sights, smells, taste, language, and ritual.' Amid all of her efforts to exoticize sushi, Freiman provided guidance on what to order and explained the difference between nigirizushi and makizushi. She then introduced six Chicago restaurants where diners could try sushi.[33]

After 1980, the year James Clavell's 1975 novel *Shōgun* became a television mini-series watched by more than 32 per cent of American households, sushi no longer needed to be defined for readers of America's major newspapers, but it still remained a food of those in the know. An article that year by Suzanne Hamlin that ran in the *Chicago Tribune* and *New York Daily News* stated that sushi 'attracts the curious, the intellectual (pure food for pure thought), the dieter, the traveller, the health nut, and the connoisseur. In other words, most people.' Hamlin counted thirty sushi bars in New York City, but at the same time noted that sushi had become even more prominent on the West Coast.

> In California, where sushi is now as rooted into the culture
> as surfing, it's called 'doing sushi', and like digital watches,
> calculators and computers, it looks like an import that is here
> to stay. And it's catching on in virtually all other urban areas.[34]

In Los Angeles, at least by the early 1980s, sushi had become pervasive in terms of restaurants and in the culture of dining out.[35] Today, California has more Japanese restaurants than any other state, according to a 2018 Japan External Trade Organization (JETRO) survey. Of the 14,129 restaurants that serve mainly Japanese food in the USA, the top states were California (4,468), New York (1,892), Florida (1,266), Washington (898) and Texas (802). My home state of Kansas was in 33rd place with 74 restaurants, while South Dakota was at the bottom with only six.[36]

The value of the cultural capital of knowledge of sushi is visible in the 1985 John Hughes film *The Breakfast Club*, where Judd Nelson's character John Bender has to ask Claire Standish, played by Molly Ringwald, what she is eating for lunch. When she replies sushi, he needs it defined for him, highlighting the difference in social status and sophistication between the effete

Roger Shimomura, *Dinner Conversation with Nancy*, 1983.

Claire and the rough bully Bender, who did not even bring his lunch. To speak for a moment about my own life, I was a high-school student at the time that *The Breakfast Club* came out, and it was the spark that provoked my friends and me to try sushi, because all of us wanted to know what the rich and popular kids did. I already knew the 1981 song 'Sushi Girl' by the San Francisco-based band The Tubes, a song with lyrics that slipped between the food sushi and a girl named Suki.

The Tubes were not the first and by no means the last to explore the double entendre possibilities of sushi and sex. Urban Dictionary contains many citations that use sushi as a substitute for various sex acts, a hot guy or a woman's genitals.[37] Such innuendos were not lost on high-school students. Note

Judd Nelson's famous reply to Molly Ringwald in *The Breakfast Club*: 'You won't accept a guy's tongue in your mouth and you are going to eat that?' *Repo Man*, a 1984 film also popular among high-school students at the time and featuring Emilio Estevez, who would later appear in *The Breakfast Club*, introduced audiences to Los Angeles punk music and to the memorable tagline 'Let's go get sushi and not pay.' The punks who aspired to sushi simultaneously rebelled against the fact that sushi was an elite food that they could not afford. In 1987 a restaurant reviewer in the *New York Times* commented, 'sushi has become the fast food of the executive set.'[38] In less than twenty years, sushi went from hippy to yuppie food.

Sushi restaurants on the West Coast enjoyed an initial geographic advantage in their ability to obtain food products from Japan and from their willingness to innovate. As early as the 1950s the Mutual Trading Company began supplying restaurants and consumers in California with Japanese products. A decade

California roll.

later, Japan Airlines began shipping from Tsukiji, Japan's main fish market in Tokyo, to America's West Coast.

Los Angeles's Little Tokyo also gave birth to the California roll in 1962, 1964 or 1971, depending on who is telling the story. Some contend that the California roll, made with avocado, imitation crab and mayonnaise, was concocted as a substitute for fish unavailable in certain months of the year. Others say that the roll was an attempt to make sushi palatable for white America, especially by turning the rice inside out to hide the nori.[39] A difficulty in trying to learn the origin of the California roll is that it is not mentioned in American newspapers until 1979, according to one scholar's survey.[40] In any event, the California roll became, for many Americans, a gateway to try Japanese food in the same way that guacamole and nachos were entry points for Mexican cuisine for the same population.[41]

Japanese restaurants were expensive in the United States until conveyor-belt sushi restaurants broadened the market. New York saw the first open in the United States in 1974, when Genroku established a branch in Manhattan. A menu dated to 1985 from Genroku on 366 Fifth Avenue preserved in the collection of the New York Public Library shows that the restaurant offered both Chinese and Japanese food. The menu advertises 'Chinese – Japanese Food on Conveyor', listing nigirizushi, beef chop suey, eggrolls (harumaki) and hot and sour soup or miso soup. The shop also sold takeaway sushi.[42] Conveyor-belt sushi offered cost-saving measures for restaurant owners, which they could pass on to customers. Customers could be served the moment that they sat down, and waiters were not needed at all, just a cashier to count the type and number of plates a customer had used.[43] With its clarity of pricing and without a potentially intimidating foreign chef to interact with, conveyor-belt sushi places offered an easy entry to the world of sushi. In 1987 the

Sushida chain of conveyor-belt sushi shops arrived in New York and within ten years had fifty outlets. Three years later, the first machine-made sushi debuted in the city at chain stores, which provided a way to keep labour costs even lower. Higher-end sushi restaurants did not lose customers to these low-cost competitors, according to Japanese restaurateur Matsumoto Hirotaka, because they targeted an upscale market.[44]

By 2003 every state in America had a Japanese restaurant and 70 per cent of these were operated by Japanese, but that number gradually changed. Today 80 per cent of Japanese restaurants in the United States are operated by non-Japanese, many of whom are Asians from other countries, including Taiwan, Thailand, Indonesia, China, South Korea, the Philippines, Cambodia and Vietnam. One reason for this shift is that the earlier generation of Japanese restaurateurs could not find successors to take on ownership of their establishments when they retired.[45] Writing broadly of ethnic succession in the restaurant trade, food studies scholar Krishnendu Ray observes that ethnic entrepreneurs initially succeeded because they could capitalize on their unique knowledge of the foods from their native lands. Ethnic chefs could also make up for a lack of capital by hard work and through the unpaid labour of relatives. Those who were successful could see their children go to college, but that step made the prospect of returning to the hard work of a restaurant less appealing for these college grads than other career paths. Consequently, many of the sons and daughters of restaurant owners left the trade for other work.[46] If the Japanese owner of a restaurant in the United States wants to hire a Japanese chef, he generally has to pay them more than chefs of other Asian countries, according to Ray. However, the main reason that non-Japanese Asians gravi-tated into the Japanese restaurant trade in the United States was because of the high level of prestige of Japanese cuisine, which

Sushi chef.

is closer to that of French or another European cuisine than to other 'ethnic' cuisines. Ray explains that 'ethnic' foods are undervalued not because of the quality of the food, but precisely when there are more people associated with that ethnicity in the United States.[47] A Filipino restaurateur can charge much more if he passes as Japanese and serves Japanese food than if he were to offer Filipino or Mexican food. Writing about the shift from Japanese sushi chefs to those of other ethnicities in recent years, Laresh Jayasanaker observes, 'while it may have been necessary at one time for a sushi bar to have a Japanese-looking person behind the counter, it was slowly becoming acceptable to have Mexican American chefs, or "susheros," crafting tuna rolls at many spots.'[48]

Non-Japanese owner-operators of restaurants in the U.S. have brought innovation but also criticism. Chinese immigrants from Fujian province came to New York in the 1980s, where many entered the restaurant business and recognized that they could sell a sushi roll for much more than an eggroll. Sushi also drew more customers than Chinese food, which suffered for its associations with frying and monosodium glutamate (MSG). These Chinese restaurateurs added sushi bars to their restaurants and created new makizushi rolls and toppings that are now the mainstay of sushi in the United States, such as the rolls that one finds in supermarkets topped with spicy mayonnaise, Chinese eel sauce, hot sauce and the like.[49] Profitable for restaurateurs, the sushi rolls served in these venues were still much less expensive for customers than the sushi in a Japanese restaurant.[50] Ogawa Hirotoshi, a chef and self-styled 'sushi samurai' who claims to have travelled to forty nations to observe conditions in Japanese restaurants, recalled the Japanese restaurants in the United States with 'locals' at the front of the house and Spanish

Red Dragon roll (shrimp tempura, tuna, avocado, red and wasabi tobiko, spicy mayo, eel sauce).

spoken at the back. While lamenting the fact that the cooking staff from Mexico and South America were underpaid, Ogawa nevertheless warned of the conditions in kitchens outside Japan operated by people who have never eaten sashimi before and 90 per cent of whom had never handled raw fish either. Ogawa reported witnessing chefs prepare fish on the same cutting boards where they had just sliced raw meat. He warned that not only did such practices increase the chance of food poisoning, they also threatened to denigrate the positive image of Japanese cuisine and sushi.[51]

Growing concerned with the rapid increase in non-Japanese-owned Japanese restaurants abroad and the quality of the food they served, in 2006 Japan's Ministry of Agriculture, Forestry and Fisheries launched a programme to certify overseas Japanese restaurants that served 'genuine' Japanese food. In American media, that initiative came to be called the 'Sushi Police'.[52] Where the 2006 certification programme failed was in the Japanese government's assertion of authority over the authenticity of Japanese restaurants abroad. However, since then (and actually well before 2006 too) the Japanese government has made an effort to gain a favourable image abroad and improve its balance of trade by promoting Japanese food internationally. A recent highpoint in these efforts was the United Nations Educational, Scientific and Cultural Organization (UNESCO) certification of the 'traditional dietary cultures of the Japanese (washoku)' in 2013.[53] Today the Japanese government supports non-governmental organizations (NGOs) to try to affect the types of food sold in Japanese restaurants outside of Japan by inviting non-Japanese restaurateurs and chefs to gain certification for their use of Japanese ingredients and for their cooking skills. Chef Ogawa Hirotoshi is the director of the World Sushi Skills Institute, 'the only sushi association credited by the Japanese government', which holds the annual Sushi Cup where chefs come to Japan to earn a 'black belt' in sushi. In cooperation with JETRO, since 2014 Ogawa also operates sushi-training workshops internationally that provide certification in sushi-making to students.[54]

The Sushi Police live on as an animated series broadcast in 2016 in Japan, showing how anxiety over non-Japanese creating Japanese food has spread to Japanese popular culture. In each five-minute episode, a three-man team of officers from the fictitious World Food Conservation Organization travel outside of Japan to discover inauthentic Japanese food. Armed with wasabi machine guns, a vacuum to collect illicit sushi and chopstick nunchaku, the Sushi Police bust illicit sushi restaurants around the globe. *Sushi Police* parodies government attempts to authenticate sushi outside of Japan, but at the same time implies that the fear of foreign sushi is justified because it is dubious, unhealthy and criminal. The fish intended to be made into this obscene non-Japanese sushi are shown weeping.[55]

SUSHI GOES GLOBAL

The establishment of Japanese restaurants in Europe followed the pattern of the United States, timed to the influx of Japanese businesses and capital, with Japanese expats opening restaurants that catered first to their compatriots before expanding their trade to other clientele.[56] In 1965 an article in *The Times* declaimed, 'in the whole of Britain there is not one restaurant specializing in Japanese meals, compared with the thousands of Indian and Chinese establishments that have shot up since the war.'[57] This absence provided the author with a reason to offer a recipe for sushi, the 'universal favourite in Japan that it is eaten at all times and at all occasions'. That recipe included Ajinomoto (aka MSG), 'the universal seasoning of Japan'.[58]

With Japanese investment, from the 1960s expats opened restaurants and brought sushi to Europe, with Asians from other countries opening their own Japanese restaurants soon after. Japanese opened the first post-war Japanese restaurant in Germany in Hamburg in 1962 and another in Düsseldorf two years later. Today, Düsseldorf has one of the largest Japanese communities in Europe, but most of the Japanese restaurants there are owned by Koreans or Chinese or by German chains.[59] These restaurants are riding the crest of the sushi boom of the 1990s, which occurred, according to food scholar Katarzyna Cwiertka, with the debut of restaurants catering to non-Japanese spurred by the prominence of sushi in American popular culture.[60]

As in the United States, conveyor-belt sushi restaurants made sushi more approachable and affordable in Europe. The first of these restaurants opened in Paris in 1984. London-developed sushi chain stores Itsu and Yo! Sushi debuted in 1997. Yo! Sushi was launched by Simon Woodroffe, who had cut his teeth staging rock concerts in London and LA. Yo! Sushi targeted the same group of trendy urbanites as Moshi Moshi, a sushi restaurant chain founded by Caroline Bennett in 1994.[61] A 2015 JETRO survey found 518 Japanese restaurants in London. Of these, 440 were sushi restaurants with 125 of them being chain stores, including Yo! Sushi with 31 stores and the Japanese-owned Sushi Bar Atari-ya with six stores.[62] In the same year, Italy had six different sushi chain restaurants with 630 Japanese restaurants total nationally.[63]

In Eastern Europe sushi came to Poland after 1990, beginning in Warsaw. From 2001 to 2014 the number of places serving sushi grew tenfold, from twelve to 120 establishments.[64] In Russia the restaurant Evraziya (Eurasia), which opened in St Petersburg in 2001, now has 100 shops, and there are 21 in Ukraine.[65]

In Hong Kong upscale Japanese restaurants were established in the 1960s to cater for Japanese working abroad, but the real take-off point for the popularization of Japanese food began in the 1980s. After the return of Hong Kong to China in 1997, eating Japanese food was one way for the people of Hong Kong to distinguish themselves from the population in mainland China.[66]

SUSHI FISHING GOES GLOBAL

As the number of Japanese restaurants has spread around the world, so has the sourcing of Japanese food, and that has changed sushi globally, particularly in Japan, where seafood has been an important part of the diet since the Jōmon period (10,000 to mid-second or first millennium BCE). Whereas the hunter-gatherer Jōmon people ate some fifty varieties of seafood, Japanese today eat around two hundred, thanks to the global reach of the Japanese fishing industry and seafood business.[67]

Commercial fishing began in Japan in the medieval period, when large-scale operations developed on Lake Biwa with fishermen who used nets and weirs to capture freshwater fish for markets in Kyoto. Ise Bay, Wakasa Bay and Izu were also important medieval fishing ports.[68] However, the take-off point for commercial fishing in Japan was the early modern period. In the seventeenth century the shogunal government invited fishermen from the Kansai area to settle in Edo, and granted fishing villages usage rights to the waters in and around Edo Bay. In return for selling part of their catch to the government at a reduced rate, the 45 fishing villages using Edo Bay paid no taxes for most of the early modern period. That law changed in 1792, but the fishing villages often still received relief from tax payments.[69]

Edo's population exceeded one million by 1700, placing greater demands on nearby waters for marine products. During the early modern period, the concept of 'before Edo' (Edomae) became a shorthand for 'fresh seafood', a term that expanded in usage from initially referring to the waters of the city's rivers and the inner bay (some 920 square km, 355 square mi.) to encompass later the Pacific coastal provinces of Sagami, Awa, Kazusa and Shimōsa provinces (modern Kanagawa, Tokushima and Chiba Prefectures).[70] Fish was an important protein source and sardines and herring were also netted to use for fertilizer.[71] The high rate of consumption of seafood in the city in the early nineteenth century made shipping fish to Edo profitable.

Laws that had prohibited deep-sea fishing in the early modern period to prevent illicit trade and secure the country's borders were eliminated in the Meiji period (1868–1912). The abolition of feudal controls on fishing left fishers unregulated in the bay and overfishing in the 1860s and '70s led to a decline in catch sizes and a sharp economic downtown for fishing villages working the bay.[72] As Japan modernized and further urbanized, the quality of Tokyo (formerly Edo) Bay's waters suffered. Urban factories polluted the bay with their emissions and tidelines were filled in, destroying the breeding grounds for many marine species. By the beginning of the twentieth century, Japan's fishermen had to chase catches further from their coast. After the First World War, Japan established tuna-fishing bases in former German colonies in the Marshall Islands, the Marianas and the Palau Islands. Diesel engines allowed Japan's fishing vessels to operate in the South China Sea and Bering Sea by the late 1930s.[73]

Notwithstanding the Second World War, which destroyed Japan's fishing fleet and ports, Japan led the world in fish landings for all but the last decade of the twentieth century, and contributed to the depletion of fish stocks initially in the Pacific Ocean and globally after the Second World War. Scholars Vaclav Smil and Kazuhiko Kobayashi provide four reasons for the expansion of Japan's industrial fishing operations from the 1950s. First, Japan rapidly developed shipbuilding operations to supply the fishing industry. Second, the inexpensive price of diesel fuel in the 1950s and '60s made long-distance fishing operations economically feasible. Third, expansion of the Japanese population provided cheap labour for fishing crews. Finally, and most critically, the oceans were ripe for exploitation given that international law held that a nation's sovereignty ended 5 kilometres (3 mi.) from their shoreline.[74] To this list one could also add advancements in refrigeration, specifically the advent of super-cooled freezers used on industrial fishing vessels, which allow fish to be preserved and brought to market at the optimal moment and condition to obtain the best prices. These developments incentivized fishing fleets to pursue bluefin and other fish high in value, allowing the emergence by the 1980s of a luxury trade for tuna in Tokyo's Tsukiji market where one fish, whether it was caught on a trawler plying equatorial waters or flown in by plane from the North Atlantic, sold for the equivalent of tens of thousands of dollars.[75] The circumstances led to the overfishing of bluefin. For example, it is estimated that in the year 2000, Japan's total catch of bluefin was three times its reported catch, the equivalent of the global catch of that species that year.[76] By the time commercial fishing ended in Tokyo Bay by 1962 and in Osaka by 1969, Japan had already developed an extensive and advanced fleet of long-range fishing boats to supply its markets with the globally highest number of landings of marine life until 1994, when it was exceeded by China.[77] By then Edomae had long only meant fresh fish, regardless of the point on the globe from which they originated.[78]

Pacific bluefin tuna.

Besides operating its own fleet, Japan imports fish globally from other producers. According to the Food and Agriculture Organization (FAO) of the United Nations, as of 2016, Japan ranked seventh in terms of global seafood landings behind China, Indonesia, India, the USA, the Russian Federation and Peru.[79] Many of these countries ship their fish to Japan, where seafood imports doubled between 1985 and 1995 and are above 3 million metric tonnes, allowing Japan's population to enjoy the highest level of seafood consumption per capita, a share roughly five times the country's share of the global population.[80] As of 2016, Japan still leads in per capita seafood consumption, but it is expected to be surpassed by China in 2026.[81]

The expansion of industrial fishing has taken a toll on marine resources and world fish stocks. A 2012 FAO report found that more than half of the globe's fishing stocks were fully exploited and almost 30 per cent were depleted or overexploited, leaving only 12.7 per cent that could be expanded.[82] Whether one explains the depletion of global fishing stocks as the 'tragedy of the commons' – in other words, the exploitation of resources that no one owns directly – or as a contradiction of capitalism in which economic activity depends upon degrading the environment in ways that undermine that very same economic activity, the fact is that global fish stocks, especially for predatory species such as bluefin tuna, are at a point of crisis.[83] In their assessment of the environmental impact of the fishing industry on bluefin stocks, Smil and Kobayashi write, 'even a complete ban on fishing in the Mediterranean and in the northeast Atlantic might not prevent an impending collapse of that fishery.'[84] Beyond bluefin, a 2019 FAO report estimated that one in five fish is taken illegally or is unreported, 'posing a serious sustainability risk to the world's oceans and to their ecosystem management'.[85]

Aquaculture is one possible solution to this dilemma. Since 1961 aquaculture has grown 3.2 per cent annually, about twice the rate of population growth; as of 2016 aquaculture accounted for $232 billion of $362 billion of global fish landings.[86] However, aquaculture does not necessarily lead to a decline in openwater fishing. 'In intensive aquaculture', writes geographer Becky Mansfield, 'fish are fed fish meal and fish oil that come from capture fisheries of wild fish. The rise of aquaculture has fuelled increased fishing activity for the low-value fish used in fish meal.' Moreover, Mansfield points out that aquaculture produces 'materially different fish' from those in the wild. Farm-raised fish are bred to be brought to market faster and have their own health issues. Farmed shrimp and salmon can be exposed to chemical fertilizers to boost levels of phytoplankton consumed by the fish. Farmed fish can encounter pesticides, anti-foulants, flocculants and disinfectants that are used to control the

Tsukiji fish market, Tokyo.

environment of the water in which they are raised. They are also sometimes given antibiotics, anti-parasite and anti-fungal medicines to keep them healthy. 'Given the potential for cumu-lative effects over the long term', Mansfield writes, 'it is difficult to conduct a risk analysis that could reasonably assert that there are (or are not) problems associated with these chemicals.'[87]

FISH, SUSHI AND GLOBAL HEALTH CONCERNS

As many commentators have noted, it is often hard for consumers to balance the health benefits of fish consumption against its possible ill effects. Yet the prevailing message for consumers is that it is better to consume some fish than not. Unfortunately, we may not know all we want to about the fish we are eating. One-third of the seafood sold in the United States is mislabelled.[88] Environmental pollution is a vast problem, and raises many questions about whether fish and sushi are safe to eat. We can raise only a few of these issues here.

The aftermath of the Fukushima nuclear accident in March 2011 prompted approximately 470,000 evacuations when the coastal region and the area surrounding the three reactors, devastated by earthquakes and a tsunami, also had to cope with the fallout of radioactive materials. On land, the Japanese government carted away topsoil and stripped the bark from trees to remove radioactive caesium, but many experts were also worried about the impact of the nuclear disaster on marine life. Radioactive nucleotides were discovered in migratory bluefin tuna caught off the coast of California in 2011. However, a study published in 2013 in the *Proceedings of the National Academy of Sciences* of the United States found that three or four times more radiation in the bluefin samples was caused by background radiation already in the environment, and that eating the tuna contaminated by the nuclear accident would mean consuming less than a dose received from a medical procedure, plane travel or by eating food items with naturally occurring nucleotides.[89] Unlike on land, ocean currents can disperse radioactive material, diluting it. High rates of caesium detected on the coast near the Fukushima site weeks after the accident have receded to lower levels. A 2016 scientific commentary in the same

Buyers and sellers at the Tsukiji fish market in Tokyo, 2012.

journal queried the risks of seafood consumption in Japan and elsewhere and found that radiation levels were very low in marine and freshwater species and posed low risks for human consumption.[90] Most of the radiation in the ocean comes from Cold War nuclear tests.[91]

In 2012, one year after the Fukushima accident, Japan revised its standards for radiation levels in food (measured in becquerels, Bq) so that they are among the most stringent globally. Japan only allows 100 Bq per kilogram of seafood, whereas the United States allowed 1,200 Bq, China 800 and South Korea 370.[92] The Japanese government has instituted a stringent testing programme for its foodstuffs, and reported that for the prefectures outside Fukushima, after September 2014 there were no samples of marine species collected that exceeded government limits; since April 2015, the same is true for Fukushima.[93] As for rice, vegetables, meat and eggs, none of the seventeen prefectures near and including Fukushima have exceeded levels for radioactivity according to government tests in 2015.[94] However, that has not convinced everyone of the safety of Japan's domestic food supply.[95]

As with radiation, microplastics are ubiquitous to the world's oceans and are raising heath concerns. A 2019 FAO report described finding microplastics in 220 different species of marine life, 55 per cent of which were commercial varieties, including mussels, oysters, Atlantic and chub mackerel, sardines and Norway lobster. However, the same report indicated a lack of data about the extent to which microplastics are dispersed in these species globally, and it stated that the health effects of consuming these have yet to be determined. Since deposits of microplastics collect in the guts of marine creatures, contamination with microplastics seems to be of most concern for smaller fish and crustaceans that are consumed whole, as opposed to larger fish in which the viscera are removed before eating. The FAO report, like most literature on potential ill effects from seafood consumption, cautions, 'On the basis of current evidence, the risk of not including fish in our diets is far greater than the risks posed by exposure to plastic-related contaminants in fish products.'[96] Still, that might provide cold comfort to those who are worried about invisible plastic particles in their seafood.

Microplastics have also been found in beer, honey, water and breast milk, but seafood is one of the main sources for exposure to mercury poisoning.[97] Mercury originates from coal-burning power plants and illegal gold mines. It is a neurotoxin, and mercury poisoning can cause muscle weakness, rashes, numbness and kidney problems, and is detrimental to brain development. Fish absorb bacteria contaminated with mercury and the mercury bioaccumulates up the food chain, so that large, predatory fish such as bluefin tuna have particularly high levels. The U.S. Food and Drug Administration (FDA) recommends that pregnant women, women who might become pregnant and women who are breastfeeding – in other words, all pre-menopausal women – limit their intake of swordfish and albacore tuna to 340 g (12 oz) a week. As Becky Mansfield observes, rather than address the problems of mercury and other pollutants in the environment, these guidelines place the burden on women to monitor their seafood intake.[98]

Another concern for seafood consumption is child labour and human trafficking. A 2018 FAO report concluded that child labour is widespread in the fishing and aquaculture sector, which employs one out of ten people globally.[99] Recent trends in the fishing industry such as illegal fishing have led to the employment of migrant workers and have facilitated human trafficking in the fishing industry, according to a 2013 International Labour Organization report. The problem is especially acute in developing nations. The report states,

> By far the most studied occurrence of forced labour and human trafficking in the fisheries sector is that which takes place in the Greater Mekong sub-Region and in particular the Thai fisheries sector.

But deceptive and coercive labour practices have also been documented in New Zealand, Russia, Turkey, South Korea, Ireland, Scotland and West Africa. In other words, forced labour in the fishing industry exists in most regions of the world and probably to a much greater extent than is known, since it goes unreported.[100]

The aforementioned issues are a concern for the fishing industry globally, but there are also specific health worries about consuming sushi. Fish used in sushi can contain roundworms, tapeworms and flukes that could be passed on to the consumer when the fish is consumed raw. However, winding up with a parasite after eating sushi seems to be extremely rare, owing to government regulations and the practices of qualified chefs. In the United States, the FDA's Hazard Analysis and Critical Control Point (HACCP) rules require that fish be frozen for sushi, such as at or below −20°C (−4°F) for seven days, long and cold enough to kill any parasites.[101] In the United Kingdom, fish for sashimi and sushi must be frozen at −20°C (−4°F) for at least 24 hours, or at −35°C (−31°F) for at least fifteen hours.[102] Long before similar regulations existed, sushi chefs endeavoured to use the freshest fish possible and examined the fish for parasites when they sliced it.[103] These practices make parasitic infections rare, although not unheard of. In Japan, cases of roundworm (*Anisakis*) infection have been reported from eating sushi.[104] Sushi and sashimi of carp and salmon can contain the larvae of tapeworms (*Diphyllobothrium latum*), and these can grow up to 10 m (33 ft) in a human intestine; however, fewer than a hundred cases are

Roundworm in salmon.

reported annually in Japan. Sweetfish sushi may have intestinal flukes, but these are usually harmless to humans.[105]

Besides the chance of catching a parasite, eating fish raw increases the chance of contracting other seafood illnesses. Fish and shellfish can carry hepatitis, E. coli infections and typhoid, all of which are caused by contaminated water. Ciguatera is one of the most common fishborne illnesses and is also the most dangerous. It is caused by a toxin created by tiny plankton in an algae bloom or red tide. Approximately 50,000 people a year are affected by ciguatera, enduring numbness that can lead to paralysis and sometimes death.[106]

Beyond potential problems with the fish, the way that sushi is made also has an impact on health. Sushi has a reputation for being healthy, but the sushi rolls that are popular in sushi restaurants, takeaway places and conveyor-belt shops globally can be deceptively high in calories, sodium and cholesterol. I recently looked at the nutritional information for two super-market chains in the U.S. Midwest and compared the contents of the makizushi with the prosaic hamburger and Big Mac from McDonald's. The results shocked me.

Dillons Dragon Roll contained twice the calories and cholesterol of a McDonald's hamburger. The sodium levels in some of the sushi are also concerning. The U.S. FDA recommends consuming no more than 2,300 mg of sodium a day, although the American Heart Association suggests no more than 1,500 mg daily.[107] The Hyvee Nori Sushi Crispy California Roll tops in at 2,020 mg of sodium, 87.8 per cent of the recommended daily value, and that is before it is dipped in soy sauce!

Unfortunately, we do not often have ready access to the nutritional information on sushi. I found some of these sushi products at one of the local branches of one of these supermar-kets, but those items did not display nutritional information on

Nutrition Content of Supermarket Sushi Rolls[108]

NAME/WEIGHT	CALORIES	SATURATED FAT (grams)	SODIUM (mg)	CHOLESTEROL (mg)
Dillons California Sushi Roll (8 oz)	460	5	1,150	10
Dillons Dragon Sushi Roll (10¾ oz)	560	4	890	65
Dillons Crunchy Roll (9 oz)	680	12	1,170	35
Hyvee Nori Sushi Crunchy California Roll (8 oz)	550	2	1,900	10
Hyvee Nori Sushi Crispy California Roll (8 oz)	640	7	2,020	10
Hyvee Nori Sushi Philadelphia Roll (7 oz)	450	7	1,190	35
McDonald's Hamburger	250	3	480	30
Big Mac	540	10	940	80

their packaging. Perhaps the fried onions, tempura toppings, sauces, mayonnaise and other ingredients should serve as enough of a warning that the sushi roll we plan to enjoy may not be very healthy after all.

A sensationalist article titled 'Sushi: The Raw Truth', appeared in the UK's *Daily Mail* in 2006 warning that 'sushi contains a cocktail of chemicals, heavy metals and pesticides which can potentially lower intelligence, reduce fertility and even lead to cancer'.[109] The article even went so far as to warn that contaminated salmon might cause 'gender bending' – 'making young boys more feminine and girls more masculine, which may also affect sexual orientation later in life'. While drawing attention to 'the polluted salmon lochs of Scotland and the filthy seas of southern Europe and the Far East', the article did not support its claims about the dangers of sushi; nor did it demonstrate that consuming sushi is any more harmful than eating other types of seafood, as in the British favourite fish and chips. While the article paints all sushi with the same brush, it is important

Grocery-store sushi from Pittsburgh, 2015.

THE GLOBAL SPREAD OF SUSHI

to remember that sushi can be made with all types of fish (or without them) and according to many different methods. As consumers, what is most important is that we become mindful of where all our food comes from, how it is produced and sold, and what effects that food has on the environment, the people who produce it and ourselves.

Rather than condemn a method of food preparation such as sushi-making out of hand, it is better to choose sushi options that are healthier for us and for the environment. We can refer to guides to sustainable fishing such as the Monterey Bay Aquarium's free Seafood Watch app, which suggests which varieties of fish are landed sustainably and which are not. Unfortunately, when we sit down to sushi we may not know if the skipjack tuna we are having was caught with trolling lines in the East Pacific or was captured by a floating-object purse seine in the Atlantic Ocean. That means that unless we trust the chef and can 'leave it to them' (*omakase*) we should be prepared to make some very specific choices when ordering sushi, avoiding bluefin tuna entirely as well as other wild and farmed fish that are not eco-certified by the Marine Stewardship Council or the Aquaculture Stewardship Council, two organizations that promote sustainable fishing and fish farming. The best choice may be to make our own makizushi and fill our rolls with what we like and know is good.

CHIRASHIZUSHI WITH SUMMER VEGETABLES

(2 servings)

This is a vegetarian version of chirashizushi that often changes in my home depending on what is on hand.

2 cups [480 ml] cooked short-grain rice
vinegar (rice or apple cider vinegar preferred)
2 teaspoons sugar
½ teaspoon salt

For the kinshi tamago (shredded egg):
2 eggs
1 teaspoon sugar
pinch of salt
oil

Vegetables:
1 cup [240 ml] boiled corn (fresh or frozen)
½ cup [120 ml] salted cucumber: about half a cucumber;
½ teaspoon salt
½ cup [120 ml] boiled edamame (fresh or frozen)
1 sliced avocado
5 halved cherry tomatoes
lightly boiled and sliced okra (optional)
pickled lotus root (optional): small lotus root 2 inches [5 cm]
in length; 1 cup [240 ml] water; 1 teaspoon vinegar for boiling
and 1 teaspoon for marinade; 1 tablespoon sugar;
1 teaspoon salt
pickled ginger (optional)
thinly chopped shiso (optional)

Make the salted cucumber and pickled lotus roots in advance.

Salted cucumber

Wash and slice half of a cucumber and cut it as thin as possible. Sprinkle salt and let it sit for at least 30 minutes. Squeeze any water from the cucumber.

Pickled lotus

Wash and peel off the skin, then slice the lotus root thinly. Add vinegar into boiling water. Boil the lotus for 3 minutes. Make a vinegar mixture by adding water, vinegar, sugar and salt in a small bowl. Soak the cooked lotus in the mixture for at least 1 hour.

Mix a tablespoon of vinegar, the sugar and salt in a large bowl. Transfer the hot, cooked rice into the vinegar mixture. Mix it gently. Let it rest for 30 minutes to cool to room temperature. While the rice cools, make the shredded eggs (kinshi tamago)

Kinshi tamago

Beat eggs; add the sugar and salt. Heat a non-stick pan on medium heat. Apply a thin layer of vegetable oil to the pan. Pour a small amount of egg mixture into the pan and swirl it around as if making a thin crepe. Lower the heat and wait until the egg has solidified. If it looks uncooked, flip it over and cook for a few more seconds. Transfer to a plate. Make 3–4 and stack them up. When they are cool, roll them up and cut into thin strips.

Divide the rice into two shallow bowls and top with all the ingredients.

Sushi Doughnut at Chotto Matte, Soho, London. Chef: Jordan Sclare.

SIX
SUSHI TOMORROW?

Two millennia ago, sushi – or what the Chinese called *zha* and *zhi* – was fish fermented in salt with or without rice; today, those same characters, as well as the English word sushi, refer to a plethora of ways to prepare not just fish but all sorts of foods to the point that it is hard to understand what ties them all together apart from their shared name. Only a fraction of the sushi made today undergoes months of lactic-acid fermentation, as the millennia-old sushi created in ancient China and in premodern Japan did, and yet sushi is still being made. Today, the most widely available sushi is the sushi roll, makizushi, which chefs put anything in, anything on top of and have even reconstructed into bagel, doughnut and pizza shapes. Some may argue that a sushi bagel is not authentic; however, the history of sushi is one of transformation, not stasis. Recipes for sushi have changed more than they have remained the same, otherwise we would all have to wait several months to eat sushi, from the time we began a sushi recipe to the time that the fish had finished fermenting and was ready for consumption.

Sushi is a remarkable food also for the fact that it does not have a sole inventor. The transformation from sushi made with lactic-acid fermentation (narezushi) to namanare, sushi eaten before the fish is fully fermented, to 'fast sushi' (hayazushi) in which sake, kōji and vinegar were added to facilitate fermentation so that the sushi could be eaten sooner, were all key stages in the development of sushi and were the work of anonymous chefs and home cooks tinkering with widely known ways in which fish can be preserved and its flavour enhanced by packing it with rice and salt, and waiting. Even the descendants of Hanaya Yohe'e, who is often credited with inventing nigirizushi, asserted only that he refined the recipe. The Japanese had a long tradition of pressing fish on rice, so limiting the rice to smaller portions able to carry a sliver of fish is a natural extension of a widely practised cooking method. Today, makizushi has become the basis for experimentation, with variations such as the California roll, whose relatively short history has already become impossible to trace.

Even what is said to be Japan's oldest form of sushi, the funazushi of Lake Biwa, is evolving. In researching this book, I had the opportunity to visit a store near the shores of Lake Biwa that is turning funazushi into sandwiches and desserts. The small cafe and delicatessen Biwako Daughters located in Yasu, Shiga Prefecture, is a family operation that makes funazushi and other traditional fish products, but it is also transforming these recipes into something new as a way to broaden the audience for traditional foods. One of these innovations was a funazushi sandwich made with a slice of funazushi and creamy Dutch cheese between crusty Italian bread. Funazushi can be quite salty and very sour, but inside the sandwich the fermented fish transforms into a prosciutto taste that reminded me of a sandwich I enjoyed once in a quiet hilltop café in Tuscany. Except,

Funazushi sandwich.

instead of some luscious but unidentified Italian sausage, the main ingredient was fermented crucian carp. Dessert brought an even bigger surprise when the cafe owner, Ms Nagakawa Tomomi, cut a *meron* bread in half and filled it with cream. The cocoa-flavoured sweet was a variation on the usual meron bread recipe that is a golden bun with a cookie-dough topping which crackles and turns yellow in the oven so that the sweet resembles its namesake, a musk melon. This meron bread was a dark chocolate but the truly magical part was the cream, sweetened and turned slightly lemony thanks not to any citrus but to a tablespoon of the rice used for making funazushi that had been added to it. Funazushi itself is an acquired taste best consumed in small bites as an accompaniment to sake or beer, but the funazushi sandwich would appeal to anyone who loves a good sandwich. One wonders – and I hope – that the next chapter in sushi's development might see a return to sushi's roots as a slow food but one finding new expression in ways suited to modern palates, whether in Japan where rice consumption per

Meron bread with funazushi cream.

capita is half of what it was fifty years ago and more people than ever before are turning to bread, or outside of that country where sandwiches have historically inspired as much culinary experimentation as, well, sushi.

Funazushi sandwiches might also serve as muse to solving problems with invasive species in Japan and elsewhere. Bluegills, native to North America, were introduced to Japan some fifty years ago and have multiplied exponentially in some of Japan's waterways. Lake Biwa had a population of 25 million bluegill in 2007, according to one estimate. Among the many responses to curbing the fish were the efforts of one company that tried to make lactic-acid sushi from bluegill following a similar recipe to funazushi.[1] In the United States, bighead carp, black carp, grass carp and silver carp – known collectively as Asian carp – arrived forty years ago with the hopes that with their voracious appetites they could control weeds in canal systems and aquatic farms. But, like the bluegill in Japan, the carp escaped into local waterways, including the Mississippi River, where they now crowd out other fish for space and food. Asian carp are edible and since the fish are vegetarians they are safer to eat than predatory fish, which have higher levels of mercury from consuming smaller prey. However, carp has a negative image in the United States. Carp sound too ornamental and too close to goldfish, something only swallowed by intoxicated fraternity pledges decades ago. In response, some marketers have redubbed Asian carp as 'silver fin' and 'Kentucky white fish' in the same move that lured people dubious of dolphin fish to try eating Atlantic mahi-mahi.[2] A silver fin sushi sandwich has an alliterative appeal that I hope prompts someone to make it a reality. For people in the American Midwest, rather than eat imported and endangered bluefin tuna, it makes more sense to try to make a local sushi with a fish that is in overabundance in nearby rivers. In other words, in an age of diminishing resources and concerns about fossil fuel use, rather than think in terms

Asian carp leaping.

PACIFIC SAURY SUSHI (SANMAZUSHI)

Using frozen Pacific saury purchased from an Asian market in Kansas City, we are able to replicate at home this traditional sushi recipe from Mie and Wakayama Prefectures.

One Pacific saury (raw or frozen): you can judge the freshness of the fish by making sure that its eyes are not cloudy. A fish that is not too oily is best for this recipe.

For the fish
1 teaspoon salt
2 tablespoons rice or apple cider vinegar
Fresh lime juice (optional)

For the sushi rice
1 cup [240 ml] cooked rice
1–1½ tablespoons vinegar
2 teaspoons sugar
½ teaspoon salt

Cut off the head and clean the fish, removing the spine and internal organs, scales and veins. Wash thoroughly. Dry the fish and flatten it so that the interior cavity is exposed. Sprinkle on the salt. Cover the fish with plastic wrap on a plate and place it in the refrigerator for about a day.

Take out the fish from the refrigerator, and remove any smaller bones. Pour vinegar on the fish to wash off most of the salt, and then drain off the vinegar. Sprinkle on the lime juice (and more vinegar if desired). Cover the fish again with plastic wrap and return it to the refrigerator for about half a day.

Cook the rice as usual and while it is still warm mix in the vinegar, sugar and salt. Allow the rice to cool.

With the interior of the fish facing upwards, fill the cavity with rice evenly. Place the fish on some plastic wrap and use that to press the rice into the cavity of the fish so that the fish regains its original shape.

Leave the fish wrapped for 30 minutes to an hour in the refrigerator. Remove the plastic wrap and slice the fish crosswise into about five pieces, and serve.

Sanmazushi, a sushi using Pacific saury, is made by marinating a whole salted fish in vinegar and yuzu, then packing the cavity of the fish with rice. It is a local delicacy in Mie and Wakayama prefectures.

of Edomae as the pinnacle of freshness and import fish from halfway around the globe from Japan, it would be better for us, wherever we are, to search for our own local-mae (my mae?) and make that the basis for our sushi.

As sushi consumers – fans? lovers? – we will quibble about our favourites, but if we hope to continue to enjoy sushi, it is important that we make our decisions to do so mindfully, endeavouring to choose sustainable seafood, visiting establishments where the sushi chefs are knowledgeable and the other workers earn a living wage, and appreciating sushi for its long history, which may be rooted in Asia, but which is now global.

GLOSSARY

chirashizushi: see gomokuzushi.

futomaki (太巻): a large makizushi; see makizushi.

gomokuzushi (五目鮨): literally, 'five item' sushi, which is similar to scattered sushi (散らしずし chirashizushi or ばらずし barazushi), in which sliced fish and other ingredients are placed on top of or mixed in rice flavoured with vinegar, salt and a sweetener.

hakozushi (箱鮨): 'box sushi', also called 'pressed sushi' (oshizushi, 押鮨), a speciality of Osaka. Sushi ingredients are placed together inside a lidded box and then formed together by applying pressure with the lid.

hayazushi (早鮨): 'quick sushi' that developed around the late 1600s, a type of namanare that usually adds vinegar (or sometimes sake, kōji or sake lees) to hasten the fermentation process to a few days.

inarizushi (稲荷鮨): a fried tofu skin folded around a ball of sweet sushi rice is the most typical example today.

kōji (麹、糀): a mould that is used in sake making to break down the sugars in rice so that they are available for fermentation. Kōji can refer both to the mould purchased as a powder and to rice that has been treated with it. In sushi-making, kōji is introduced to facilitate the fermentation process of some namanare sushi.

kokerazushi (柿鮨): 'shingle sushi', a variety that developed in the late medieval period featuring sashimi on top of rice. Tekone sushi (手捏ね鮨) in Mie Prefecture is a modern example.

makizushi (巻ずし): sushi rolls; typically made with nori seaweed (and so called norimaki) but can also be made with konbu or egg wrappers. Invented in Edo in the late eighteenth century.

namanare (生成/生熟, fresh matured sushi): a variety of narezushi that matures for much less time, allowing the rice to be more easily eaten with the fish. Namanare sushi developed in the latter part of the Muromachi era (1336–1573). Today, it is found in Wakayama Prefecture featuring mackerel (*saba*) and is made with sweetfish (ayu) throughout Japan.

narezushi (馴鮨, fully fermented sushi): the most ancient form of sushi. Salted fish are packed with rice and pressed for months, if not years. The rice becomes porridge-like and it is usually discarded but the fish is sliced and eaten bones and all. The crucian carp sushi (funazushi) of Shiga Prefecture is the representative example today.

neta: see *tane*.

nigirizushi (握り鮨): debuted in Edo (Tokyo) by the early nineteenth century, it is also sometimes called Edomaezushi, 'sushi using seafood caught near Edo', thus synonymous with fresh sushi. The familiar and ubiquitous sushi of rice topped with sliced fish. The thinly sliced fish is pressed on the rice by hand.

norimaki: see makizushi.

oshizushi: see hakozushi.

sugatazushi (姿鮨): 'whole sushi', also known as 'poll sushi' (*bōzushi* 棒ずし), an entire fish stuffed with rice. The fish is gutted, salted, then stuffed with rice flavoured with vinegar. It is then wrapped in bamboo grass and placed in a box, where it is pressed down with a heavy weight for between an hour and a day until the flavours of the fish and rice blend. The mackerel (saba) and pike conger (hamo) sushi of Kyoto, and sweetfish sushi of Yoshino in Nara, are typical examples.

tane (種、タネ) (sometimes reversed as *neta* ネタ): the toppings and ingredients used in sushi.

unohanazushi (卯の花ずし): *unohana* means deutzia, a genus of flowering plant, but here it is a euphemism for tofu lees (okara), the mashed soybeans left over from making tofu that are often fried and made into a salad by adding sliced mushrooms and vegetables. Unohanazushi uses tofu lees instead of rice. Several examples of local sushi in Hiroshima use tofu lees.

REFERENCES

INTRODUCTION: WHAT IS SUSHI?

1 Hsing-Tsung Huang, *Science and Civilization in China*, vol. VI: *Biology and Biological Technology, Part V: Fermentation and Food Science* (Cambridge, 2000), p. 385.
2 Hibino Terutoshi, *Sushi no rekishi o tazuneru* (Tokyo, 1999), pp. 125–6.
3 Regarding the controversies around the California roll, see Robert Ji-Song Ku, *Dubious Gastronomy: The Cultural Politics of Eating Asian in the USA* (Honolulu, HI, 2014), pp. 17–48. The ingredients of these various rolls are as described in Ōkawa Tomohiko, *Gendai sushigaku sushiology: Sushi no rekishi to sushi no ima ga wakaru* (Tokyo, 2008), p. 456.
4 James Farrer et al., 'Japanese Culinary Mobilities: The Multiple Globalizations of Japanese Cuisine', in *Routledge Handbook of Food in Asia*, ed. Cecilia Leong-Salobir (London, 2019), pp. 39–57, p. 48.
5 Ogawa Hirotoshi, *Sushi samurai ga iku! Toppu sushi shokunin ga sekai o mawariaruite mite kita* (Tokyo, 2018), pp. 78–80.
6 'Bratislava Lends its Name to Sushi Rolls', *Slovak Spectator*, 28 November 2016, p. 13.
7 Sugino Gonuemon, *Meihan burui*, in *Nihon ryōri hiden shūsei: Genten gendaigoyaku*, vol. IX, ed. Issunsha (Kyoto, 1985), pp. 211–72, p. 268.
8 Ibid., p. 268.
9 Ōkawa, *Gendai sushigaku sushiology*, p. 2.

10 Hibino Terutoshi, *Sushi no kao: Jidai ga motometa aji no kakumei* (Tokyo, 1997), pp. 18–19.

11 Ōkawa, *Gendai sushigaku sushiology*, p. 57.

12 Hibino, *Sushi no kao*, p. 15.

13 Huang, *Science and Civilization in China*, p. 384.

14 Hayakawa Hikari, *Nihon ichi Edomaezushi ga wakaru hon* (Tokyo, 2009), p. 29.

15 Harold McGee, *On Food and Cooking: The Science and Lore of the Kitchen, Completely Revised and Updated* (New York, 2004), pp. 44–5; Huang, *Science and Civilization in China*, p. 380.

16 Matsushita Sachiko, *Zusetsu Edo ryōri jiten* (Tokyo, 1996), p. 40.

17 Shinoda Osamu, *Sushi no hon* (Tokyo, 2002), p. 23.

18 Okumura Ayao, 'Kaisetsu', in *Sushi narezushi*, in *Kikigaki furusato katei ryōri*, vol. 1, ed. Nōsan Gyoson Bunka Kyōkai (Tokyo, 2002), pp. 235–53, p. 242.

19 Hashimoto Michinori, ed., *Saikō funazushi no rekishi* (Hikone, 2016), p. 274.

20 'Funazushiyō no oke Kiso Sawara-sei', www.kiso2.com, accessed 16 June 2020.

21 Hibino, *Sushi no rekishi o tazuneru*, p. 29.

22 Hashimoto, *Saikō funazushi no rekishi*, p. 275.

23 Chieko Fujita, 'Funa Zushi', The Tokyo Foundation, www.tkfd.or.jp, accessed 16 June 2020.

24 Hibino, *Sushi no rekishi o tazuneru*, p. 63; Shinoda, *Sushi no hon*, pp. 22–3.

25 Sugino, *Meihan burui*, p. 269.

26 Kate Springer, 'Narezushi: A Taste of Ancient Sushi in Japan', CNN, cnn.com, 10 January 2018.

27 Hibino, *Sushi no rekishi o tazuneru*, p. 34.

28 *Gōrui nichiyō ryōrishō*, in *Nihon ryōri hiden shūsei: Genten gendaigoyaku*, vol. 1, ed. Issunsha (Kyoto, 1985), pp. 95–217, p. 171.

29 Ibid., p. 170.

30 Matsushita Sachiko and Yoshikawa Seiji, 'Koten ryōri no kenkyū (2): Ryōri anbaishū ni tsuite', *Chiba daigaku kyōiku gakubu kenkyū kiyō*, XXV/2 (1975), pp. 166–218, p. 200.

31 See the separate chapters on medieval and early modern funazushi in Hashimoto, *Saikō funazushi no rekishi*, pp. 101–41, 149–91.

32 Santōsha, *Shokuseikatsu dēta sōgō tōkei nenpyō 2016* (Tokyo, 2016), pp. 265–6.

33 Naruse Uhei, *Yonjū nana todōfuken: Gyoshoku bunka hyakka* (Tokyo, 2011), p. 10.

34 Craig Claiborne, 'For Feasting on Sushi, There's a Restaurant in Osaka', *New York Times*, 10 December 1968, p. 52.

35 Sasha Issenberg, *The Sushi Economy: Globalization and the Making of a Modern Delicacy* (New York, 2007).

36 Theodore C. Bestor, *Tsukiji: The Fish Market at the Center of the World* (Berkeley, CA, 2004).

37 Trevor Corson, *The Zen of Fish: The Story of Sushi, from Samurai to Supermarket* (New York, 2007).

38 Eric C. Rath, *Food and Fantasy in Early Modern Japan* (Berkeley, CA, 2010), pp. 121–65.

39 Hibino, *Sushi no kao*, p. 106.

40 Okumura Ayao, 'Kaisetsu', p. 236.

41 Meguro Hidenobu, *Sushi no gijutsu taizen* (Tokyo, 2013), pp. 48–251.

42 Ōkawa, *Gendai sushigaku sushiology*, pp. 195–285.

43 Ibid., pp. 295, 297.

ONE SEARCHING FOR THE ORIGINS OF SUSHI

1 Hsing-Tsung Huang, *Science and Civilisation in China*, vol. VI: *Biology and Biological Technology*, Part V: *Fermentation and Food Science* (Cambridge, 2000), p. 379.

2 Ibid., pp. 384–6.

3 Hibino Terutoshi, *Sushi no rekishi o tazuneru* (Tokyo, 1999), p. 27.

4 Japanese commentators identify this as *Perilla citriodora*, a plant similar to the perilla but with a lemon fragrance. Tanaka Seiichi, Kojima Re'eitsu and Ōta Yasuhiro, eds, *Semin yōjutsu: Genson suru saiko no ryōrisho* (Tokyo, 1997), p. 104.

5 Huang, *Science and Civilisation in China*, p. 555.

6 Tada Taeko and Imai Kunikatsu, *Satoyama no sansai: Ko no mi handobukku* (Tokyo, 2013), pp. 146–7.

7 Richard Hosking, *A Dictionary of Japanese Food: Ingredients and Culture* (Rutland, VT, 1996), pp. 124–5.

8 Huang, *Science and Civilisation in China*, p. 174.

9 Tanaka, Kojima and Ōta, eds, *Semin yōjutsu*, p. 173.

10 Huang, *Science and Civilisation in China*, pp. 388–90.

11 Ishige Naomichi and Kenesu Raduru, *Gyoshō to narezushi no kenkyū: Monsūn Ajia no shokuji bunka* (Tokyo, 1990), p. 53.

12 I am grateful to Q. Edward Wang for telling me the meaning of this term.

13 Q. Edward Wang, *Chopsticks: A Cultural and Culinary History* (Cambridge, 2015), pp. 27, 30; Tanaka, Kojima and Ōta, eds, *Semin yōjutsu*, p. 221.

14 Ibid., p. 141.

15 Shinoda Osamu, *Sushi no hon* (Tokyo, 2002), pp. 152–3, 155; Hibino, *Sushi no rekishi o tazuneru*, p. 26.

16 As discussed in Ōkawa Tomohiko, *Gendai sushigaku sushiology: Sushi no rekishi to sushi no ima ga wakaru* (Tokyo, 2008), pp. 48–50.

17 Hibino, *Sushi no rekishi o tazuneru*, p. 27; Ōkawa Tomohiko, *Gendai sushigaku sushiology*, p. 59.

18 Emiko Ohnuki-Tierney, *Rice as Self: Japanese Identities Through Time* (Princeton, NJ, 1993), p. 33.

19 Hibino Terutoshi, *Sushi no kao: Jidai ga motometa aji no kakumei* (Tokyo, 1997), pp. 27–8, 31–4; Ishige and Raduru, *Gyoshō to narezushi no kenkyū*, p. 13.

20 Charlotte von Verschuer, *Rice, Agriculture, and the Food Supply in Premodern Japan*, trans. and ed. Wendy Cobcroft (London, 2016), pp. 4, 231, 300.

21 Ibid., p. 11.

22 Ibid., pp. 180–81.

23 Hibino, *Sushi no kao*, p. 28.

24 Nōsan Gyoson Bunka Kyōkai, ed., *Sushi narezushi*, in *Kikigaki furusato katei ryōri* (Tokyo, 2002), vol. 1, pp. 62, 194, 104–7, 144.

25 Sugino Gonuemon, *Meihan burui*, in *Nihon ryōri hiden shūsei: Genten gendaigoyaku*, vol. IX, ed. Issunsha (Kyoto, 1985), pp. 211–72, p. 272.

26 Harada Nobuo, *Edo no ryōrishi: Ryōribon to ryōri bunka* (Tokyo, 1989), p. 128.

27 Sugino, *Meihan burui*, p. 260.

28 Ibid., p. 272.

29 Cited in Okuyama Masurō, *Mikaku hyōgen jiten: Nihon ryōri* (Tokyo, 2001), p. 382.

30 This omission may be because urine does not have a consistent taste. Medical doctors in the West from the age of Hippocrates to the Victorian period relied on a flavour wheel to help diagnose a patient's condition in light of the colour or taste of their urine. Nicola Twilley, 'Urine Flavour Wheels', www.ediblegeography.com, accessed 28 March 2019.

31 I appreciate Tae-ho Kim and Kyoungjin Bae informing me about this Korean dish.

32 Andrea Osimani et al., 'Unveiling Hákarl: A Study of the Microbiota of the Traditional Icelandic Fermented Fish', *Food Microbiology*, LXXXII (2019), pp. 560–72, p. 561.

33 Ōkawa, *Gendai sushigaku sushiology*, pp. 57–8.

34 Shinoda, *Sushi no hon*, pp. 190–91.

35 Hibino, *Sushi no kao*, pp. 46–7.

36 Ōkawa, *Gendai sushigaku sushiology*, pp. 57–8, 64–5.

37 Von Verschuer, *Rice, Agriculture, and the Food Supply in Premodern Japan*, p. 13.

38 Hibino, *Sushi no rekishi o tazuneru*, p. 39.

39 Yunoki Manabu, *Sakezukuri no rekishi, shinsōpan* (Tokyo, 2005), p. 13.

40 *Konjaku monogatarishū*, vol. IV, ed. Mabuchi Kazuo, Kunisaki Fumimaro and Inagaki Tai'ichi, in *Shinpen Nihon koten bungaku taikei*, vol. XXXVIII (Tokyo, 1999), pp. 570–71.

TWO SUSHI IN THE MEDIEVAL AGE

1 *Shijōryū hōchōsho*, in *Nihon ryōri hiden shūsei: Genten gendaigoyaku*, vol. XVIII, ed. Issunsha (Kyoto, 1985), pp. 47–69, p. 52.

2 Charlotte von Verschuer, *Rice, Agriculture, and the Food Supply in Premodern Japan*, trans. and ed. Wendy Cobcroft (London, 2016), p. 76.

3 Hibino Terutoshi, *Sushi no rekishi o tazuneru* (Tokyo, 1999), p. 50.

4 Shinoda Osamu, *Sushi no hon* (Tokyo, 2002), pp. 38, 40–42.

5 Shōsekiken Sōken, *Ryōri mōmoku chōmishō*, in *Nihon ryōri hiden shūsei: Genten gendaigoyaku*, vol. II, ed. Issunsha (Kyoto, 1985), pp. 219–323, pp. 288–9.

6 *Ryōri monogatari*, in *Nihon ryōri hiden shūsei: Genten gendaigoyaku*, vol. I, ed. Issunsha (Kyoto, 1985), pp. 5–92, p. 86.

7   Ebara Kei, Ryōri monogatari kō: Edo no aji konjaku (Tokyo, 1991),
    p. 18.
8   Hibino, Sushi no rekishi o tazuneru, p. 63.
9   Ryōri monogatari, p. 87.
10 Shinoda, Sushi no hon, pp. 200–201, 206; Hibino Terutoshi, Sushi
    no kao: Jidai ga motometa aji no kakumei (Tokyo, 1997), pp. 33, 61.
11 Shijōryū hōchōsho, p. 59.
12 For a description of these inedible culinary displays, see Eric
    C. Rath, Food and Fantasy in Early Modern Japan (Berkeley, CA, 2010),
    pp. 76–9.
13 Ryōri no sho, in Nihon ryōri hiden shūsei: Genten gendaigoyaku,
    vol. XVIII, ed. Issunsha (Kyoto, 1985), pp. 145–64, p. 148.
14 For a description of 'knife ceremonies', see Rath, Food and Fantasy
    in Early Modern Japan, pp. 38–51.
15 Shijōryū hōchōsho, p. 65.
16 Hōchō kikigaki, in Nihon ryōri hiden shūsei: Genten gendaigoyaku,
    vol. XVIII, ed. Issunsha (Kyoto, 1985), pp. 87–96, p. 87.
17 Sasaki Michio, Yakiniku no bunkashi: Yakiniku, horumon, naizō to
    shinjitsu (Tokyo, 2012), p. 69.
18 Okada Tetsu, Tabemono no kigen jiten (Tokyo, 2013), p. 279.
19 Kinoshita Masashi, 'Manyō jidai no shokuseikatsu', in Tabemono
    no kōkogaku, ed. Kawano Shinjirō, Kinoshita Masashi and Tamura
    Koichi (Tokyo, 2007), pp. 85–133, p. 87.
20 Naruse Uhei, Yonjū nana todōfuken: Gyoshoku bunka hyakka
    (Tokyo, 2011), p. 12.
21 Shijōryū hōchōsho, p. 61.
22 Ibid., pp. 51–2, 61–2.
23 Ryōri no sho, p. 159.
24 Shijōryū hōchōsho, pp. 52, 64.
25 Ryōri no sho, p. 159.
26 Ehara Ayako, Ishikawa Naoko and Higashiyotsuyanagi Shōko,
    Nihon shokumotsushi (Tokyo, 2009), pp. 138–9.
27 Naruse, Yonjū nana todōfuken: Gyoshoku bunka hyakka, p. 12.
28 Ryōri no sho, p. 160.
29 Ebara Kei, Edo ryōrishi kō: Nihon ryōri (sōsōski) (Tokyo, 1986),
    p. 115.

THREE COOKBOOKS AND STREET FOOD: SUSHI IN THE EARLY MODERN ERA

1 Conrad Totman, *Japan: An Environmental History* (New York, 2014), p. 156.
2 Iino Ryōichi, *Sushi, tempura, soba, unagi: Edo yon daimeibutsu no tanjō* (Tokyo, 2016), p. 281.
3 Sugino Gonuemon, *Meihan burui*, in *Nihon ryōri hiden shūsei: Genten gendaigoyaku*, vol. IX, ed. Issunsha (Kyoto, 1985), pp. 211–72, p. 260.
4 *Gōrui nichiyō ryōrishō*, in *Nihon ryōri hiden shūsei: Genten gendaigoyaku*, vol. I, ed. Issunsha (Kyoto, 1985), pp. 95–217, p. 216.
5 Ibid., p. 172.
6 Hibino Terutoshi, *Sushi no rekishi o tazuneru* (Tokyo, 1999), pp. 85–90.
7 Ibid., p. 173.
8 Sugino, *Meihan burui*, p. 269.
9 Since bamboo is a grass instead of a tree, 'bamboo bark' (*take no kawa*) signifies the ramentum, the brownish scales around bamboo shoots often used as a wrapper in premodern Japan.
10 Ibid., pp. 261–2, 263, 265.
11 Sugino, *Meihan burui*, p. 264.
12 Kitagawa Kisō (Morisada), *Morisada mankō*, ed. Asakura Haruhiko and Kashiwa Shūichi (Tokyo, 1992), vol. V, p. 58.
13 The annotators read the locale as Chigura, but it might refer to Chikura, now part of Kuwana City in Mie Prefecture. Sugino, *Meihan burui*, p. 261.
14 Nōsan Gyoson Bunka Kyōkai, ed., *Sushi narezushi*, in *Kikigaki furusato katei ryōri* (Tokyo, 2002), vol. I, p. 168.
15 Sugino, *Meihan burui*, p. 271.
16 Ibid., p. 266.
17 Ibid., pp. 265–6.
18 Hibino Terutoshi, *Sushi no kao: Jidai ga motometa aji no kakumei* (Tokyo, 1997), p. 117.
19 Iino, *Sushi, tempura, soba, unagi*, p. 316.
20 Ōkawa Tomohiko, *Gendai sushigaku sushiology: Sushi no rekishi to sushi no ima ga wakaru* (Tokyo, 2008), p. 191; Hibino surmises that makizushi developed as a variation of sugatazushi, given that early recipes suggest that makizushi was pressed in a box like

sugatazushi and cut into slices the same way. Hibino Terutoshi, *Nihon sushi kikō: Makizushi to inarizushi to Sukeroku to* (Tokyo, 2018), pp. 36, 39.

21 Kitagawa, *Morisada mankō*, vol. v, p. 59.

22 Hibino, *Sushi no rekishi o tazuneru*, pp. 129–30.

23 Miyoshi Ikkō, *Edo seigyō bukka jiten* (Tokyo, 2002), pp. 140, 375.

24 Sugino, *Meihan burui*, p. 262.

25 Ibid., pp. 262–3.

26 Ōkawa, *Gendai sushigaku sushiology*, pp. 186–7, 192–3.

27 Ibid., p. 95.

28 Hibino, *Nihon sushi kikō*, pp. 16–17.

29 Ibid., pp. 49, 52–3.

30 Hibino, *Sushi no rekishi o tazuneru*, p. 129.

31 Iino, *Sushi, tempura, soba, unagi*, pp. 154–5, 158–60.

32 Roderick I. Wilson, 'Placing Edomae: The Changing Environmental Relations of Tokyo's Early Modern Fishery', *Resilience: A Journal of the Environmental Humanities*, III (2015–16), pp. 242–89, pp. 261, 272–3.

33 Hibino, *Sushi no rekishi o tazuneru*, pp. 159–60.

34 Koizumi Seizaburō, *Katei sushi no tsukekata* (Tokyo, 1910), p. 158.

35 Hibino, *Sushi no kao*, p. 107; Ōkawa, *Gendai sushigaku sushiology*, p. 100.

36 Koizumi, *Katei sushi no tsukekata*, p. 159.

37 Kitagawa, *Morisada mankō*, vol. v, p. 58.

38 Akano Hirofumi, '"Narezushi" kara "Edomaezushi" e no shinka to sono fukugen ni tsuite', *Nihon chōri kagaku kaishi*, XLI/3 (2008), pp. 214–16.

39 Hibino, *Sushi no kao*, p. 118.

40 Kitagawa, *Morisada mankō*, vol. v, p. 59.

41 Harada Nobuo, 'Edo no tabemonoya: Furiuri kara ryōrijaya made', in *Rakugo ni miru Edo no shokubunka*, ed. Tabi no Bunka Kenkyūkaijo (Tokyo, 2000), pp. 105–27, p. 117.

42 Iino Ryōichi, *Sushi, tempura, soba, unagi*, pp. 214, 227, 236, 316. For an overview of the history of tempura, see Eric C. Rath, *Food and Fantasy in Early Modern Japan* (Berkeley, CA, 2010), pp. 103–6.

43 Eric C. Rath, 'The Tastiest Dish in Edo: Print, Performance, and Culinary Culture in Early Modern Japan', *East Asian Publishing and Society*, III/2 (2013), pp. 184–214, p. 210.

FOUR SUSHI IN MODERN JAPAN, FROM SNACK TO DELICACY

1 Tōkyō Gurakubu, *Saishin Tōkyō annai* (Tokyo, 1907), pp. 41–2, 45.

2 The chub mackerel is usually described as *Scomber japonicus*. Taizo Fujimoto, *The Nightside of Japan* (London, 1915), p. 38.

3 Ōkawa Tomohiko, *Gendai sushigaku sushiology: Sushi no rekishi to sushi no ima ga wakaru* (Tokyo, 2008), pp. 116–17.

4 Koizumi Seizaburō, *Katei sushi no tsukekata* (Tokyo, 1910), p. 172.

5 Ibid., pp. 173–4.

6 Shūkan Asahi, ed., *Shin nedan no fūzokushi: Meiji, Taishō, Shōwa* (Tokyo, 1990), p. 185.

7 Tōkyō Shoin, *Taishō eigyō benran* (Tokyo, 1914), pp. 42–3, 86–90.

8 Koizumi, *Katei sushi no tsukekata*, pp. 22–3.

9 Ibid., p. 29.

10 Ibid., pp. 89–90.

11 Ōkawa, *Gendai sushigaku sushiology*, pp. 120–21.

12 Tōkyō Shoin, *Taishō eigyō benran*, pp. 89–90.

13 Ōkawa, *Gendai sushigaku sushiology*, pp. 120–21.

14 Ibid., p. 122.

15 Yokoi Kōzō, *Roten kenkyū* (Tokyo, 1931), pp. 155–7.

16 The urban poor often bought leftover rice as that was a less expensive option than preparing it at home, which required equipment and fuel. See James L. Huffman, *Down and Out in Late Meiji Japan* (Honolulu, HI, 2018), pp. 111–12.

17 Ishizumi Harunosuke, *Asakusa keizaigaku* (Tokyo, 1933), pp. 160–76.

18 Kon Tōji, *Famrirī resutoran: 'Gaishoku' no kingendaishi* (Tokyo, 2003), p. 44.

19 Matsuzaki Tenmin, *Tōkyō tabearuki*, republished in *Gurume annaiki*, ed. Kondō Hiroko (Tokyo, 2005), pp. 1–132, p. 100.

20 Ibid., pp. 68, 100.

21 *Yomiuri shimbun*, 24 May 1925, p. 11, accessed through Yomidasu Rekishikan, https://databaseyomiuri.co.jp, 26 June 2019.

22 Matsuzaki, *Tōkyō tabearuki*, p. 100.

23 Ibid.

24 Akano Hirofumi, '"Narezushi" kara "Edomaezushi" e no shinka to sono fukugen ni tsuite', *Nihon chōri kagagaku kaishi*, XLI/3 (2008), pp. 214–17, p. 215.

25 Yomiuri shimbun, 22 July 1931, p. 7. Accessed through Yomidasu Rekishikan, https://database.yomiuri.co.jp, 26 June 2019.

26 Matsuzaki, Tōkyō tabearuki, pp. 101–2.

27 Calculated with reference to George Solt, The Untold History of Ramen: How Political Crises in Japan Spawned a Global Food Craze (Berkeley, CA, 2014), p. 20.

28 Shiraki Masamitsu, Dai Tōkyō umaimono tabearuki, republished in Gurume annaiki, ed. Kondō Hiroko (Tokyo, 2005), pp. 135–644, pp. 162–3.

29 Ibid., pp. 385, 392, 403–4.

30 Ibid., pp. 601–2.

31 Nagase Ganosuke, Sushi tsū (Tokyo, 1984), pp. 116–17, 121.

32 Hibino, Sushi no kao, p. 133.

33 Kon, Famrirī resutoran, p. 70.

34 Katarzyna J. Cwiertka, Cuisine, Colonialism and Cold War: Food in Twentieth-century Korea (London, 2012), p. 22.

35 Hibino, Sushi no kao, p. 135.

36 Ōkawa, Gendai sushigaku sushiology, pp. 122–3.

37 Ogawa Hirotoshi, Sushi samurai ga iku! Toppu sushi shokunin ga sekai o mawariaruite mite kita (Tokyo, 2018), p. 170.

38 Seijō Daigaku Minzokugaku Kenkyūjo, ed., Nihon no shokubunka: Shōwa shoki, zenkoku shokuji shūzoku no kiroku (Tokyo, 1990), p. xi. For a discussion of the larger findings of this survey, see Eric C. Rath, Japan's Cuisines: Food, Place and Identity (London, 2016), pp. 137–42.

39 Seijō Daigaku Minzokugaku Kenkyūjo, ed., Nihon no shokubunka, p. 372.

40 Ibid., pp. 242, 346.

41 Ibid., pp. 152, 216, 306, 321, 402.

42 The modern recipe for sake sushi combines rice and ingredients such as bamboo shoots, cloud ear fungus, carrots, shiitake, shrimp and perilla leaves in a barrel over which a sweet local sake is drizzled. Ōkawa, Gendai sushigaku sushiology, p. 356.

43 Seijō Daigaku Minzokugaku Kenkyūjo, ed., Nihon no shokubunka hoi hen: Shōwa shoki, zenkoku shokuji shūzoku no kiroku (Tokyo, 1995), p. 244; Seijō Daigaku Minzokugaku Kenkyūjo, ed., Nihon no shokubunka, pp. 14, 294, 549.

44 Seijō Daigaku Minzokugaku Kenkyūjo, ed., *Nihon no shokubunka*,
    pp. 358, 392; Seijō Daigaku Minzokugaku Kenkyūjo, ed., *Nihon no
    shokubunka hoi hen*, pp. 85, 176.
45 Seijō Daigaku Minzokugaku Kenkyūjo, ed., *Nihon no shokubunka*,
    pp. 106–7, 180, 207, 258, 607; Seijō Daigaku Minzokugaku
    Kenkyūjo, ed., *Nihon no shokubunka hoi hen*, p. 100.
46 Seijō Daigaku Minzokugaku Kenkyūjo, ed., *Nihon no shokubunka
    hoi hen*, p. 118; Seijō Daigaku Minzokugaku Kenkyūjo, ed., *Nihon
    no shokubunka*, pp. 70, 232, 414.
47 B. F. Johnston, *Japanese Food Management in World War Two* (Palo
    Alto, CA, 1953), p. 85; Takeuchi Yukiko, 'Chōri to jendā', in
    Shokubunka kara shakai ga wakaru!, ed. Yano Keiichi (Tokyo, 2009),
    pp. 101–46, p. 122.
48 Simon Partner, *Toshié: A Story of Village Life in Twentieth-century
    Japan* (Berkeley, CA, 2004), p. 133.
49 For a discussion of the revival of local foods as local cuisines
    from the 1960s, see Rath, *Japan's Cuisines*, pp. 154–64.
50 Ōkawa, *Gendai sushigaku sushiology*, p. 341.
51 Santōsha, *Shokuseikatsu dēta sōgō tōkei nenpyō 2016* (Tokyo, 2016),
    p. 266.
52 Hashimoto Kenji, *Izakaya horoyoi kōgengaku* (Tokyo, 2014), pp. 100,
    103, 108.
53 Sasaki Michio, *Yakiniku no bunkashi: Yakiniku, horumon, naizō to
    shinjitsu* (Tokyo, 2012), p. 87.
54 Ōkawa, *Gendai sushigaku sushiology*, p. 123; Shinoda Osamu, *Sushi no
    hon* (Tokyo, 2002), pp. 84–5.
55 Jordan Sand, 'How Tokyo Invented Sushi', in *Food and the City*, ed.
    Dorothée Imbert (Washington, DC, 2014), pp. 231–2.
56 Vaclav Smil and Kazuhiko Kobayashi, *Japan's Dietary Transition and
    Its Impacts* (Cambridge, MA, 2012), p. 182.
57 For a discussion of this book, see Rath, *Japan's Cuisines*, pp. 156–7.
58 Nakagawa Noriko, *Nihon no kyōdo ryōri* (Tokyo, 1974), pp. 30, 69.
59 Ōkawa, *Gendai sushigaku sushiology*, pp. 392–3.
60 Ibid., pp. 388–9.
61 Ogawa, *Sushi samurai ga iku!*, p. 37.
62 Ibid., pp. 22–3.
63 Hirotaka Matsumoto, *Nyū Yōku Takesushi monogatari* (Tokyo, 1995),
    p. 78.

64 Katarzyna J. Cwiertka, 'From Ethnic to Hip: Circuits of Japanese Cuisine in Europe', *Food and Foodways*, XIII/4 (2005), pp. 241–72, pp. 254, 255.
65 Theodore C. Bestor, 'Kaiten-zushi and Konbini: Japanese Food Culture in the Age of Mechanical Reproduction', in *Fast Food/ Slow Food: The Cultural Economy of the Global Food System*, ed. Richard Wilk (Lanham, MD, 2006), pp. 115–30, p. 120.
66 Kon, *Famrirī resutoran*, pp. 249–50; Agence France-Presse, 'Yoshiaki Shiraishi, 87, Sushi Innovator', *New York Times*, www.nytimes.com, 31 August 2001.
67 Ōkawa, *Gendai sushigaku sushiology*, p. 131.
68 Santōsha, *Shokuseikatsu dēta sōgō tōkei nenpyō 2016*, p. 262.
69 Ogawa, *Sushi samurai ga iku!*, p. 27.
70 Gaishoku Sangyō o Tsukutta Hitobito Henshū Iinkai, ed., *Gaishoku sangyō o tsukutta hitobito* (Tokyo, 2005), pp. 185–92.
71 'Kigyō gaiyō', https://kozosushi.co.jp, accessed 15 June 2020.
72 Yoshioka Yō, 'Kozōzushi ga utsusu, "mochikaeri sushi" gyōtai no genkai', *Nikkei bijinesu*, 29 March 2019, accessed through https://business.nikkei.com, 15 July 2019.
73 Santōsha, *Shokuseikatsu dēta sōgō tōkei nenpyō 2016*, p. 263.
74 Smil and Kobayashi, *Japan's Dietary Transition and Its Impacts*, pp. x, 2, 36–7, 94, 189.
75 Lindsay Whipp, 'The Sushi Summit: Obama in Japan', *Financial Times*, www.ft.com, 23 April 2014.
76 *Michelin Guide*, cited through https://gm.gnavi.co.jp, accessed 15 June 2020.
77 'Dining at Jiro', www.sushi-jiro.jp, accessed 15 June 2020.

FIVE THE GLOBAL SPREAD OF SUSHI

1 Statistics Bureau of Japan, www.stat.go.jp, accessed 23 August 2019. I appreciate the help of James Farrer and Michiko Ito in navigating this database.
2 Ministry of Agriculture, Forestry and Fisheries, 'Kaigai ni okeru Nihon resutoran no kazu', www.maff.go.jp, accessed 22 July 2019; Ministry of Agriculture, Forestry and Fisheries, 'Kaigai ni okeru Nihon resutoran no kazu (2017 nen)', in Santōsha, *Shokuseikatsu dēta sōgō tōkei nenpyō 2019* (Tokyo, 2019), p. 186.

3 James Farrer et al., 'Japanese Culinary Mobilities: The Multiple
   Globalizations of Japanese Cuisine', *Routledge Handbook of Food in
   Asia*, ed. Cecilia Leong-Salobir (London, 2019), pp. 39–57, p. 41.
4 'Eel, Seaweed in Sandwich', *Los Angeles Times*, 29 December 1957,
   p. D8.
5 Theodore C. Bestor, 'How Sushi Went Global', *Foreign Policy*,
   no. 121 (2000), pp. 54–63, p. 57.
6 Ujita Norihiko, *Amerika ni Nihonshoku bunka o kaikasaseta
   samuraitachi* (Tokyo, 2008), p. 141.
7 Koyama Shūzō, 'Nihon ryōriten no rekishi to bunpu', in
   Rosuanjerusu no Nihon ryōriten: Sono bunka jinruigaku kenkyū, ed.
   Ishige Naomichi et al. (Tokyo, 1985), pp. 25–47, pp. 26–8.
8 Ōkawa Tomohiko, *Gendai sushigaku sushiology: Sushi no rekishi to
   sushi no ima ga wakaru* (Tokyo, 2008), p. 124.
9 Senkichiro Katsumata, *Notes on Japanese Cuisine* (Tokyo, 1946), p. 2.
10 Koyama, 'Nihon ryōriten no rekishi to bunpu', p. 33.
11 Ibid., p. 32.
12 Welly Shibata, 'Chords and Discords', *Shin Sekai*, 14 May 1932,
   https://hojishinbun.hoover.org, accessed 20 November 2019.
13 'Sushi House in New Location', *The Rafu Shimpo*, 6 October 1933,
   p. 6, accessed through www.eastview.com, 4 October 2019.
14 National Park Service, 'Little Tokyo Historic District',
   www.nps.gov, accessed 22 November 2019.
15 Tsuyoshi Matsumoto, 'We Want Show Windows for Showing',
   The Rafu Shimpo, 2 April 1940, accessed through www.eastview.
   com, 4 October 2019.
16 Koyama, 'Nihon ryōriten no rekishi to bunpu', p. 36.
17 Matsumoto Hirotaka, *Nyū Yōku Takesushi monogatari* (Tokyo, 1995),
   p. 28.
18 Hui Manaolana, *Japanese Foods (Tested Recipes)* (Honolulu, HI,
   1956), pp. 56, 110, 112.
19 Craig Claiborne, 'Restaurants on Review: Variety of Japanese
   Dishes Offered, But Raw Fish is Specialty on Menu', *New York
   Times*, 11 November 1963, p. 37; Craig Claiborne, 'New Yorkers
   Take to Tempura and Chopsticks With Gusto', *New York Times*,
   10 March 1966, p. 22.

20 Hui Manaolana, *Japanese Foods (Tested Recipes)*, pp. 10, 34, 37.

21 Matsumoto, *Nyū Yōku Takesushi monogatari*, pp. 28–9.

22 Kay Loring, 'Front Views and Profiles', *Chicago Tribune*, 8 March 1968, p. C3.

23 Trevor Corson, *The Zen of Fish: The Story of Sushi, from Samurai to Supermarket* (New York, 2007), p. 46.

24 Ujita, *Amerika ni Nihonshoku bunka o kaikasaseta samuraitachi*, p. 142. Ishige Naomichi dates the appearance of a sushi case in 'restaurant K' in Little Tokyo to 1962. Ishige Naomichi, 'Nihon shokuhin kyōkyū suru hitobito', in *Rosuanjerusu no Nihon ryōriten: Sono bunka jinruigaku kenkyū*, ed. Ishige Naomichi et al. (Tokyo, 1985), pp. 195–208, p. 202.

25 Koyama, 'Nihon ryōriten no rekishi to bunpu', pp. 37, 39.

26 Matsumoto, *Nyū Yōku Takesushi monogatari*, pp. 138–9.

27 Craig Claiborne, 'For Feasting on Sushi, There's a Restaurant in Osaka', *New York Times*, 10 December 1968, p. 52.

28 Craig Claiborne, 'The Wonders of Sushi', *Chicago Tribune*, 10 July 1975, p. A10.

29 Matsumoto, *Nyū Yōku Takesushi monogatari*, p. 80.

30 Andrew Gordon, *A Modern History of Japan: From Tokugawa Times to the Present*, 3rd edn (New York, 2014), pp. 290–91.

31 Krishnendu Ray, 'Ethnic Succession and the New American Restaurant Cuisine', in *The Restaurants Book: Ethnographies of Where We Eat*, ed. David Beriss and David Sutton (New York, 2007), pp. 97–114, p. 103.

32 Barry Hillenbrand, 'From the Folks Who Brought You Sony Comes a Fishy Ritual in the Raw', *Chicago Tribune*, 24 March 1980, pp. E1–2.

33 Jane Salzfass Freiman, 'Sushi: A "Fast-Food" Fish Dish from Japan', *Chicago Tribune*, 12 May 1978, pp. B1, B3–B4.

34 Suzanne Hamlin, 'Sushi: A Japanese Import That's Here to Stay', *Chicago Tribune*, 25 September 1980, p. B17E.

35 Sasha Issenberg, *The Sushi Economy: Globalization and the Making of a Modern Delicacy* (New York, 2007), p. 99.

36 Japan External Trade Organization (JETRO), 'Heisei sanjūnendo Beikoku ni okeru Nihonshoku resutoran dōkō chōsa', 2018, www.jetro.go.jp.

37 'Sushi', Urban Dictionary, www.urbandictionary.com, accessed 30 July 2019.

38 Bryan Miller, 'One Old-timer, One Just Opened', *New York Times*, 24 July 1987, p. c26.

39 Farrer et al., 'Japanese Culinary Mobilities: The Multiple Globalizations of Japanese Cuisines', pp. 45, 47; Robert Ji-Song Ku, *Dubious Gastronomy: The Cultural Politics of Eating Asian in the USA* (Honolulu, HI, 2014), pp. 44–7.

40 Jonas House, 'Sushi in the United States, 1945–1970', *Food and Foodways*, XXVI/1 (2018), pp. 40–62, p. 58.

41 Ku, *Dubious Gastronomy*, p. 22.

42 'Genroku Sushi Restaurant [Menu]', 1985, New York Public Library, http://menus.nypl.org, accessed 11 July 2019.

43 Issenberg, *The Sushi Economy*, pp. 72–3.

44 Matsumoto, *Nyū Yōku Takesushi monogatari*, pp. 189–90.

45 JETRO, 'Heisei sanjūnendo Beikoku ni okeru Nihonshoku resutoran dōkō chōsa', 2018, www.jetro.go.jp.

46 Ray, 'Ethnic Succession and the New American Restaurant Cuisine', p. 112.

47 Krishnendu Ray, *The Ethnic Restaurateur* (London, 2016), pp. 82–3, 108.

48 Laresh Jayasanker, *Sameness in Diversity: Food and Globalization in Modern America* (Berkeley, CA, 2020), p. 15.

49 Farrer et al., 'Japanese Culinary Mobilities: The Multiple Globalizations of Japanese Cuisines', p. 48.

50 James Farrer et al., 'Japanese Culinary Mobilities Research: The Globalization of the Japanese Restaurant', *Foods and Food Ingredients*, CCXXII/3 (2017), pp. 256–66, p. 260.

51 Ogawa Hirotoshi, *Sushi samurai ga iku! Toppu sushi shokunin ga sekai o mawariaruite mite kita* (Tokyo, 2018), pp. 14, 15, 38.

52 Rumi Sakamoto and Matthew Allen, 'There's Something Fishy About That Sushi: How Japan Interprets the Global Sushi Boom', *Japan Forum*, XXIII/1 (2011), pp. 99–121, pp. 108–11.

53 Eric C. Rath, *Japan's Cuisines: Food, Place and Identity* (London, 2016), pp. 17–33.

54 World Sushi Skills Institute, https://wssi.jp, accessed 12 July 2019.

55 Sushi Police, http://sushi-police.com, accessed 26 July 2019.

56 Farrer et al., 'Japanese Culinary Mobilities: The Multiple Globalizations of Japanese Cuisine', p. 46.
57 JETRO, 'Eikoku (Rondon) ni okeru Nihonshoku resutoran jittai chōsa: Nihon resutoran no intabyū kara', 2015, www.jetro.go.jp.
58 'Eating Japanese', *The Times*, 26 July 1965, p. 13, The Times Digital Archive, www.gale.com/c/the-times-digital-archive, accessed 11 July 2019.
59 Farrer et al., 'Japanese Culinary Mobilities Research', p. 260.
60 Katarzyna J. Cwiertka, 'From Ethnic to Hip: Circuits of Japanese Cuisine in Europe', *Food & Foodways*, XIII/4 (2005), pp. 241–72, pp. 256–7.
61 Ibid., pp. 256–7.
62 JETRO, 'Eikoku (Rondon) ni okeru Nihonshoku resutoran jittai chōsa', 2015, www.jetro.go.jp.
63 JETRO, 'Itaria (Mirano) ni okeru Nihonshoku resutoran jittai chōsa: Nihon resutoran no intabyū kara', 2015, www.jetro.go.jp.
64 Ewa Czarniecka-Skubina and Dorota Nowak, 'Japanese Cuisine in Poland: Attitudes and Behaviour Among Polish Consumers', *International Journal of Consumer Studies*, XXXVIII/1 (2014), pp. 62–8, p. 63.
65 Farrer et al., 'Japanese Culinary Mobilities Research', p. 261.
66 Yoshiko Nakano, 'Eating One's Way to Sophistication: Japanese Food, Transnational Flows, and Social Mobility in Hong Kong', in *Transnational Trajectories in East Asia: Nation, Citizenship, and Region*, ed. Y. N. Soysal (New York, 2014), pp. 106–29, pp. 108, 110, 114.
67 Naruse Uhei, *Yonjūnana todōfuken gyoshoku bunka hyakka* (Tokyo, 2011), p. 3.
68 Conrad Totman, *Japan: An Environmental History* (New York, 2014), p. 138.
69 Jordan Sand, 'How Tokyo Invented Sushi', in *Food and the City*, ed. Dorothée Imbert (Washington, DC, 2014), pp. 223–48, p. 234.
70 Roderick I. Wilson, 'Placing Edomae: The Changing Environmental Relations of Tokyo's Early Modern Fishery', *Resilience: A Journal of the Environmental Humanities*, III (2015–16), pp. 242–89, p. 261.
71 Harada Nobuo, *Edo no shokuseikatsu* (Tokyo, 2003), pp. 190, 194.
72 Sand, 'How Tokyo Invented Sushi', p. 239.

73 Vaclav Smil and Kazuhiko Kobayashi, *Japan's Dietary Transition and Its Impacts* (Cambridge, MA, 2012), p. 177.

74 Ibid., pp. 174, 175.

75 Sand, 'How Tokyo Invented Sushi', p. 244.

76 Smil and Kobayashi, *Japan's Dietary Transition and Its Impacts*, p. 180.

77 Totman, *Japan: An Environmental History*, pp. 207, 267–8; Smil and Kobayashi, *Japan's Dietary Transition and Its Impacts*, p. 174.

78 Wilson, 'Placing Edomae', pp. 269, 273.

79 Food and Agriculture Organization of the United Nations (FAO), *Fishery and Aquaculture Statistics 2016* (Rome, 2018), p. 9, www.fao.org.

80 Smil and Kobayashi, *Japan's Dietary Transition and Its Impacts*, p. 179.

81 Food and Agriculture Organization of the United Nations (FAO), 'Europe, the Ocean and Feeding the World', 20 March 2018, www.fao.org.

82 Cited in International Labour Organization, 'Caught at Sea: Forced Labour and Trafficking in Fisheries', pp. 4–5, www.ilo.org, accessed 30 July 2019.

83 Both views are explained in Becky Mansfield, 'Is Fish Health Food or Poison? Farmed Fish and the Material Production of Un/Healthy Nature', *Antipode*, XLIII/2 (2010), pp. 413–34.

84 Smil and Kobayashi, *Japan's Dietary Transition and Its Impacts*, p. 184.

85 Food and Agriculture Organization of the United Nations (FAO), 'Increasing Transparency of Fisheries to Enhance Sustainability of Oceans and Ecosystem Management', 2019, www.fao.org.

86 Food and Agriculture Organization of the United Nations (FAO), 'Impacts of Climate Change on Fisheries and Agriculture', 2019, www.fao.org.

87 Mansfield, 'Is Fish Health Food or Poison?', pp. 420, 423, 426–8.

88 Shingo Hamada and Richard Wilk, *Seafood: Ocean to the Plate* (New York, 2019), p. 119.

89 Nicholas S. Fisher et al., 'Evaluation of Radiation Doses and Associated Risk from the Fukushima Nuclear Accident to Marine Biota and Human Consumers of Seafood', *Proceedings of the National Academy of Sciences*, CX/26 (2013), pp. 10670–75.

90 Mark P. Little et al., 'Measurement of Fukushima-related Radioactive Contamination in Aquatic Species', *Proceedings of the National Academy of Sciences*, CXIII/14 (2016), pp. 3720–21.

91 Marcus Woo, 'Food in Fukushima Is Safe, but Fear Remains', *Wired Magazine*, www.wired.com, 12 March 2015.

92 Ministry of Health, Labour and Welfare, 'Post 3/11: Food Safety in Japan', www.mhlw.go.jp, accessed 23 November 2016.

93 The report does acknowledge that, since 2017, for freshwater species eight samples from Fukushima and three from other prefectures have exceeded limits. See Ministry of Agriculture, Forestry and Fisheries, 'FY 2017 Trends in Fisheries: FY 2018 Fisheries Policy White Paper on Fisheries: Summary', p. 26, www.maff.go.jp, accessed 1 August 2019.

94 Ministry of Agriculture, Forestry and Fisheries, 'FY 2015 Annual Report on Food, Agriculture and Rural Areas in Japan', 2016, p. 35, www.maff.go.jp. It should be noted that references to radiation testing are not mentioned in the FY 2017 and FY 2018 reports.

95 For a study of those dissenting voices, see Aya Hirata Kimura, *Radiation Brain Moms and Citizen Scientists: The Gender Politics of Food Contamination After Fukushima* (Durham, NC, 2016).

96 Food and Agriculture Organization of the United Nations (FAO), 'Microplastics in Fisheries and Aquaculture', 2019, www.fao.org.

97 Ibid.; Becky Mansfield, 'Environmental Health as Biosecurity: "Seafood Choices", Risk, and the Pregnant Woman as Threshold', *Annals of the Association of American Geographers*, CII/5 (2012), pp. 969–76, p. 970.

98 Mansfield, 'Is Fish Health Food or Poison?', pp. 424–5.

99 Food and Agriculture Organization of the United Nations (FAO), 'Eliminating Child Labour in Fisheries and Aquaculture: Promoting Decent Work and Sustainable Fish Value Chains', 2018, www.fao.org.

100 International Labour Organization, 'Caught at Sea: Forced Labour and Trafficking in Fisheries', pp. v, 14.

101 Malden C. Nesheim and Ann L. Yaktine, eds, *Seafood Choices: Balancing Benefits and Risks* (Washington, DC, 2007), pp. 166, 168.

102 Food Standards Agency, 'Freezing Fish and Fishery Products', www.food.gov.uk, accessed 13 December 2019.

103 Hamada and Wilk, *Seafood*, p. 10.

104 Yosho Fukita, Tsutoshi Asaki and Yoshiki Katakura, 'Some Like It Raw: An Unwanted Result of a Sushi Meal', *Gastroenterology*, CXLVI/5 (2014), pp. E8–E9.

105 Yukifumi Nawa, Christoph Hatz and Johannes Blum, 'Sushi Delights and Parasites: The Risk of Fishborne and Foodborne Parasitic Zoonoses in Asia', *Clinical Infectious Diseases*, XLI/9 (2005), pp. 1297–1303, pp. 1297, 1298, 1301.

106 For a catalogue of the major diseases from eating fish and shellfish, see Hamada and Wilk, *Seafood*, pp. 5–7, 9.

107 American Heart Association, 'How Much Sodium Should I Eat Per Day', www.heart.org, accessed 1 August 2019.

108 The information in this table is from the following websites: Dillons Food Stores, www.dillons.com, accessed 31 July 2019; Hyvee Aisle Online, www.hy-vee.com, accessed 20 June 2020; www.mcdonalds.com, accessed 31 July 2019.

109 Danny Penman, 'Sushi: The Raw Truth', *Daily Mail*, 4 April 2006, p. 41.

SIX SUSHI TOMORROW?

1 Yomiuri Shimbun, 'Japanese Urged to Eat Troublesome Bluegills', 23 November 2007, republished in *East Bay Times*, www.eastbaytimes.com, accessed 7 August 2019.

2 Nick Visser, 'Eat the Enemy: The Delicious Solution to Menacing Asian Carp', *Huffington Post*, www.huffpost.com, 6 December 2016.

SELECT BIBLIOGRAPHY

Akano Hirofumi, '"Narezushi" kara "Edomaezushi" e no shinka to
   sono fukugen ni tsuite', *Nihon chōri kagaku kaishi*, XLI/3 (2008),
   pp. 214–17
Bestor, Theodore C., 'How Sushi Went Global', *Foreign Policy*, 121
   (2000), pp. 54–63
—, 'Kaiten-zushi and Konbini: Japanese Food Culture in the Age
   of Mechanical Reproduction', in *Fast Food/Slow Food: The Cultural
   Economy of the Global Food System*, ed. Richard Wilk (Lanham, MD,
   2006), pp. 115–30
—, *Tsukiji: The Fish Market at the Center of the World* (Berkeley, CA, 2004)
Corson, Trevor, *The Zen of Fish: The Story of Sushi, from Samurai to
   Supermarket* (New York, 2007)
Cwiertka, Katarzyna J., *Cuisine, Colonialism and Cold War: Food in
   Twentieth-century Korea* (London, 2012)
—, 'From Ethnic to Hip: Circuits of Japanese Cuisine in Europe',
   Food and Foodways, XIII/4 (2005), pp. 241–72
Czarniecka-Skubina, Ewa, and Dorota Nowak, 'Japanese Cuisine in
   Poland: Attitudes and Behaviour Among Polish Consumers',
   International Journal of Consumer Studies, XXXVIII/1 (2014), pp. 62–8
Ebara Kei, *Edo ryōrishi kō: Nihon ryōri (sōsōski)* (Tokyo, 1986)
—, *Ryōri monogatari kō: Edo no aji konjaku* (Tokyo, 1991)
Ehara Ayako, Ishikawa Naoko and Higashiyotsuyanagi Shōko, *Nihon
   shokumotsushi* (Tokyo, 2009)

Farrer, James et al., 'Japanese Culinary Mobilities: The Multiple
    Globalizations of Japanese Cuisine', in *Routledge Handbook of Food
    in Asia*, ed. Cecilia Leong-Salobir (London, 2019), pp. 39–57
—, 'Japanese Culinary Mobilities Research: The Globalization of the
    Japanese Restaurant', *Foods & Food Ingredients*, CCXXII/3 (2017), pp.
    256–66
Fisher, Nicholas S., et al., 'Evaluation of Radiation Doses and
    Associated Risk from the Fukushima Nuclear Accident to
    Marine Biota and Human Consumers of Seafood', *Proceedings
    of the National Academy of Sciences*, CX/26 (2013), pp. 10670–75
Food and Agriculture Organization of the United Nations (FAO),
    'Eliminating Child Labour in Fisheries and Aquaculture:
    Promoting Decent Work and Sustainable Fish Value Chains',
    2018, www.fao.org
—, 'Europe, the Ocean and Feeding the World', 20 March 2018,
    www.fao.org
—, *Fishery and Aquaculture Statistics 2016* (Rome, 2018), www.fao.org
—, 'Impacts of Climate Change on Fisheries and Agriculture', 2019,
    www.fao.org
—, 'Increasing Transparency of Fisheries to Enhance Sustainability
    of Oceans and Ecosystem Management', 2019, www.fao.org
—, 'Microplastics in Fisheries and Aquaculture', 2019, www.fao.org
Fujimoto, Taizo, *The Nightside of Japan* (London, 1915)
Fujita, Chieko, 'Funa Zushi', *The Tokyo Foundation*, www.tkfd.or.jp,
    accessed 10 June 2020
Fukita, Yosho, Tsutoshi Asaki and Yoshiki Katakura, 'Some Like
    It Raw: An Unwanted Result of a Sushi Meal', *Gastroenterology*,
    CXLVI/5 (2014), pp. E8–E9
Gaishoku Sangyō o Tsukutta Hitobito Henshū Iinkai, ed., *Gaishoku
    sangyō o tsukutta hitobito* (Tokyo, 2005)
Gordon, Andrew, *A Modern History of Japan: From Tokugawa Times to the
    Present*, 3rd edn (New York, 2014)
Gōrui nichiyō ryōrishō, in *Nihon ryōri hiden shūsei: Genten gendaigoyaku*,
    vol. I, ed. Issunsha (Kyoto, 1985), pp. 95–217
Hamada, Shingo, and Richard Wilk, *Seafood: Ocean to the Plate* (New
    York, 2019)
Harada Nobuo, *Edo no ryōrishi: Ryōribon to ryōri bunka* (Tokyo, 1989)
—, *Edo no shokuseikatsu* (Tokyo, 2003)

—, 'Edo no tabemonoya: Furiuri kara ryōrijaya made', in *Rakugo ni
    miru Edo no shokubunka*, ed. Tabi no Bunka Kenkyūkaijo (Tokyo,
    2000), pp. 105–27
Hashimoto Kenji, *Izakaya no sengoshi* (Tokyo, 2014)
—, *Izakaya no sengoshi* (Tokyo, 2015)
Hashimoto Michinori, ed., *Saikō funazushi no rekishi* (Hikone, 2016)
Hayakawa Hikari, *Nihon ichi Edomaezushi ga wakaru hon* (Tokyo, 2009)
Hibino Terutoshi, *Nihon sushi kikō: Makizushi to inarizushi to Sukeroku to*
    (Tokyo, 2018)
—, *Sushi no kao: Jidai ga motometa aji no kakumei* (Tokyo, 1997)
—, *Sushi no rekishi o tazuneru* (Tokyo, 1999)
Hirotaka Matsumoto, *Nyū Yōku Takesushi monogatari* (Tokyo, 1995)
Hōchō kikigaki, in *Nihon ryōri hiden shūsei: Genten gendaigoyaku*, vol. XVIII,
    ed. Issunsha (Kyoto, 1985), pp. 87–96
Hosking, Richard, *A Dictionary of Japanese Food: Ingredients and Culture*
    (Rutland, VT, 1996)
House, Jonas, 'Sushi in the United States, 1945–1970', *Food and
    Foodways*, XXVI/1 (2018), pp. 40–62
Huang, Hsing-Tsung, *Science and Civilisation in China*, vol. VI: *Biology
    and Biological Technology, Part V: Fermentation and Food Science*
    (Cambridge, 2000)
Huffman, James L., *Down and Out in Late Meiji Japan* (Honolulu, HI,
    2018)
Hui Manaolana, *Japanese Foods (Tested Recipes)* (Honolulu, HI, 1956)
Iino Ryōichi, *Sushi, tempura, soba, unagi: Edo yon daimeibutsu no tanjō*
    (Tokyo, 2016)
Ishige Naomichi, 'Nihon shokuhin kyōkyū suru hitobito', in
    Rosuanjerusu no Nihon ryōriten: Sono bunka jinruigaku kenkyū, ed.
    Ishige Naomichi et al. (Tokyo, 1985), pp. 195–208
Ishige Naomichi and Kenesu Raduru, *Gyoshō to narezushi no kenkyū:
    Monsūn Ajia no shokuji bunka* (Tokyo, 1990)
Ishizumi Harunosuke, *Asakusa keizaigaku* (Tokyo, 1933)
Issenberg, Sasha, *The Sushi Economy: Globalization and the Making of a
    Modern Delicacy* (New York, 2007)
Japan External Trade Organization (JETRO), 'Eikoku (Rondon) ni
    okeru Nihonshoku resutoran jittai chōsa: Nihon resutoran no
    intabyū kara', 2015, www.jetro.go.jp

—, 'Heisei sanjūnendo Beikoku ni okeru Nihonshoku resutoran dōkō chōsa', 2018, www.jetro.go.jp

Jayasanker, Laresh, *Sameness in Diversity: Food and Globalization in Modern America* (Berkeley, CA, 2020)

Johnston, B. F., *Japanese Food Management in World War Two* (Palo Alto, CA, 1953)

Katsumata, Senkichiro, *Notes on Japanese Cuisine* (Tokyo, 1946)

Kimura, Aya Hirata, *Radiation Brain Moms and Citizen Scientists: The Gender Politics of Food Contamination After Fukushima* (Durham, NC, 2016)

Kinoshita Masashi, 'Manyō jidai no shokuseikatsu', in *Tabemono no kōkogaku*, ed. Kawano Shinjirō, Kinoshita Masashi and Tamura Koichi (Tokyo, 2007), pp. 85–133

Kitagawa Kisō (Morisada), *Morisada mankō*, ed. Asakura Haruhiko and Kashiwa Shūichi (Tokyo, 1992), 5 vols

Koizumi Seizaburō, *Katei sushi no tsukekata* (Tokyo, 1910)

Kon Tōji, *Famrirī resutoran: 'Gaishoku' no kingendaishi* (Tokyo, 2003)

Konjaku monogatarishū, vol. IV, in *Shinpen Nihon koten bungaku taikei*, vol. XXXVIII, ed. Mabuchi Kazuo, Kunisaki Fumimaro and Inagaki Tai'ichi (Tokyo, 2002)

Koyama Shūzō, 'Nihon ryōriten no rekishi to bunpu', in *Rosuanjerusu no Nihon ryōriten: Sono bunka jinruigaku kenkyū*, ed. Ishige Naomichi et al. (Tokyo, 1985), pp. 25–47

Ku, Robert Ji-Song, *Dubious Gastronomy: The Cultural Politics of Eating Asian in the USA* (Honolulu, HI, 2014)

Little, Mark P., et al., 'Measurement of Fukushima-related Radioactive Contamination in Aquatic Species', *Proceedings of the National Academy of Sciences*, CXIII/14 (2016), pp. 3720–21

Mansfield, Becky, 'Environmental Health as Biosecurity: "Seafood Choices", Risk, and the Pregnant Woman as Threshold', *Annals of the Association of American Geographers*, CII/5 (2012), pp. 969–76

—, 'Is Fish Health Food or Poison? Farmed Fish and the Material Production of Un/Healthy Nature', *Antipode*, XLIII/2 (2010), pp. 413–34

Matsumoto Hirotaka, *Nyū Yōku Takesushi monogatari* (Tokyo, 1995)

Matsushita Sachiko, *Zusetsu Edo ryōri jiten* (Tokyo, 1996)

Matsushita Sachiko and Yoshikawa Seiji, 'Koten ryōri no kenkyū (2): Ryōri anbaishū ni tsuite', *Chiba daigaku kyōiku gakubu kenkyū kiyō*, XXV/2 (1975), pp. 166–218

Matsuzaki Tenmin, *Tōkyō tabearuki*, republished in *Gurume annaiki*,
    ed. Kondō Hiroko (Tokyo, 2005), pp. 1–132
Meguro Hidenobu, *Sushi no gijutsu taizen* (Tokyo, 2013)
Ministry of Agriculture, Forestry and Fisheries (MAFF), 'FY 2015
    Annual Report on Food, Agriculture and Rural Areas in Japan'
    (2016), www.maff.go.jp, accessed 1 August 2019
—, 'FY 2017 Trends in Fisheries: FY 2018 Fisheries Policy White Paper
    on Fisheries: Summary', www.maff.go.jp, accessed 1 August 2019
—, 'Kaigai ni okeru Nihon resutoran no kazu', www.maff.go.jp,
    accessed 22 July 2019
Miyoshi Ikkō, *Edo seigyō bukka jiten* (Tokyo, 2002)
Nagase Ganosuke, *Sushi tsū* (Tokyo, 1984)
Nakagawa Noriko, *Nihon no kyōdo ryōri* (Tokyo, 1974)
Nakano, Yoshiko, 'Eating One's Way to Sophistication: Japanese
    Food, Transnational Flows, and Social Mobility in Hong Kong',
    in *Transnational Trajectories in East Asia: Nation, Citizenship, and Region*,
    ed. Y. N. Soysal (New York, 2014), pp. 106–29
Naruse Uhei, *Yonjūnana todōfuken: Gyoshoku bunka hyakka* (Tokyo, 2011)
Nawa, Yukifumi, Christoph Hatz and Johannes Blum, 'Sushi
    Delights and Parasites: The Risk of Fishborne and Foodborne
    Parasitic Zoonoses in Asia', *Clinical Infectious Diseases*, XLI/9 (2005),
    pp. 1297–303
Nesheim, Malden C., and Ann L. Yaktine, eds, *Seafood Choices:
    Balancing Benefits and Risks* (Washington, DC, 2007)
Nōsan Gyoson Bunka Kyōkai, ed., *Sushi narezushi*, in *Kikigaki furusato
    katei ryōri*, vol. 1 (Tokyo, 2002)
Ogawa Hirotoshi, *Sushi samurai ga iku! Toppu sushi shokunin ga sekai o
    mawariaruite mite kita* (Tokyo, 2018)
Ohnuki-Tierney, Emiko, *Rice as Self: Japanese Identities Through Time*
    (Princeton, NJ, 1993)
Okada Tetsu, *Tabemono no kigen jiten* (Tokyo, 2002)
Ōkawa Tomohiko, *Gendai sushigaku sushiology: Sushi no rekishi to sushi no
    ima ga wakaru* (Tokyo, 2008)
Okumura Ayao, 'Kaisetsu', in *Sushi narezushi*, in *Kikigaki furusato katei
    ryōri*, vol. 1, ed. Nōsan Gyoson Bunka Kyōkai (Tokyo, 2002),
    pp. 235–53
Okuyama Masurō, *Mikaku hyōgen jiten: Nihon ryōri* (Tokyo, 2001)

Osimani Andrea, et al., 'Unveiling Hákarl: A Study of the Microbiota of the Traditional Icelandic Fermented Fish', *Food Microbiology*, LXXXII (2019), pp. 560–72

Partner, Simon, *Toshié: A Story of Village Life in Twentieth-century Japan* (Berkeley, CA, 2004)

Rath, Eric C., *Food and Fantasy in Early Modern Japan* (Berkeley, CA, 2010)

—, *Japan's Cuisines: Food, Place and Identity* (London, 2016)

—, 'The Tastiest Dish in Edo: Print, Performance, and Culinary Culture in Early Modern Japan', *East Asian Publishing and Society*, III/2 (2013), pp. 184–214

Ray, Krishnendu, *The Ethnic Restaurateur* (London, 2016)

—, 'Ethnic Succession and the New American Restaurant Cuisine', in *The Restaurants Book: Ethnographies of Where We Eat*, ed. David Beriss and David Sutton (New York, 2007), pp. 97–114

Ryōri monogatari, in *Nihon ryōri hiden shūsei: Genten gendaigoyaku*, vol. I, ed. Issunsha (Kyoto, 1985), pp. 5–92

Ryōri no sho, in *Nihon ryōri hiden shūsei: Genten gendaigoyaku*, vol. XVIII, ed. Issunsha (Kyoto, 1985), pp. 145–64

Sakamoto, Rumi, and Matthew Allen, 'There's Something Fishy About That Sushi: How Japan Interprets the Global Sushi Boom', *Japan Forum*, XXIII/1 (2011), pp. 99–121

Sand, Jordan, 'How Tokyo Invented Sushi', in *Food and the City*, ed. Dorothée Imbert (Washington, DC, 2014), pp. 223–48

Santōsha, *Shokuseikatsu dēta sōgō tōkei nenpyō 2016* (Tokyo, 2016)

—, *Shokuseikatsu dēta sōgō tōkei nenpyō 2019* (Tokyo, 2019)

Sasaki Michio, *Yakiniku no bunkashi: Yakiniku, horumon, naizō to shinjitsu* (Tokyo, 2012)

Seijō Daigaku Minzokugaku Kenkyūjo, ed., *Nihon no shokubunka hoi hen: Shōwa shoki, zenkoku shokuji shūzoku no kiroku* (Tokyo, 1995)

—, *Nihon no shokubunka: Shōwa shoki, zenkoku shokuji shūzoku no kiroku* (Tokyo, 1990)

Shijōryū hōchōsho, in *Nihon ryōri hiden shūsei: Genten gendaigoyaku*, vol. XVIII, ed. Issunsha (Kyoto, 1985), pp. 47–69

Shinoda Osamu, *Sushi no hon* (Tokyo, 2002)

Shiraki Masamitsu, *Dai Tōkyō umaimono tabearuki*, republished in *Gurume annaiki*, ed. Kondō Hiroko (Tokyo, 2005), pp. 135–644

Shūkan Asahi, ed., *Shin nedan no fūzokushi: Meiji, Taishō, Shōwa* (Tokyo, 1990)

Smil, Vaclav, and Kazuhiko Kobayashi, *Japan's Dietary Transition and Its Impacts* (Cambridge, MA, 2012)

Solt, George, *The Untold History of Ramen: How Political Crises in Japan Spawned a Global Food Craze* (Berkeley, CA, 2014)

Sugino Gonuemon, *Meihan burui*, in *Nihon ryōri hiden shūsei: Genten gendaigoyaku*, vol. IX, ed. Issunsha (Kyoto, 1985), pp. 211–72

Tada Taeko and Imai Kunikatsu, *Satoyama no sansai: Ko no mi handobukku* (Tokyo, 2013)

Takeuchi Yukiko, 'Chōri to jendā', in *Shokubunka kara shakai ga wakaru!*, ed. Yano Keiichi (Tokyo, 2009), pp. 101–46

Tanaka Seiichi, Kojima Re'eitsu and Ōta Yasuhiro, eds, *Semin yōjutsu: Genson suru saiko no ryōrisho* (Tokyo, 1997)

Tōkyō Gurakubu, *Saishin Tōkyō annai* (Tokyo, 1907)

Tōkyō Shoin, *Taishō eigyō benran* (Tokyo, 1914)

Totman, Conrad, *Japan: An Environmental History* (New York, 2014)

Ujita Norihiko, *Amerika ni Nihonshoku bunka o kaikasaseta samuraitachi* (Tokyo, 2008)

von Verschuer, Charlotte, *Rice, Agriculture, and the Food Supply in Premodern Japan*, trans. and ed. Wendy Cobcroft (London, 2016)

Wang, Q. Edward, *Chopsticks: A Cultural and Culinary History* (Cambridge, 2015)

Wilson, Roderick I., 'Placing Edomae: The Changing Environmental Relations of Tokyo's Early Modern Fishery', *Resilience: A Journal of the Environmental Humanities*, vol. III (2015–16), pp. 242–89

Yokoi Kōzō, *Roten kenkyū* (Tokyo, 1931)

Yunoki Manabu, *Sakezukuri no rekishi, shinsōpan* (Tokyo, 2005)

ACKNOWLEDGEMENTS

This project began as a global history of sushi for Reaktion Books' Edible series at the initiative of publisher Michael Leaman and series editor Andy Smith. But when the final manuscript exceeded over half of its allotted word count, Michael and Andy allowed me to publish this book separately, and I appreciate their support. Reaktion's Alex Ciobanu assisted with the images; and Martha Jay, the press's managing editor, gracefully steered the book through production and helped improve it with her comments.

I would hesitate calling this book a global history because there are many parts of the world I was unable to cover. I hope to return to this topic in the future, perhaps with a team of colleagues, to chart the history and spread of sushi around the world. At that point, I would include the many images of Brazilian sushi with which my graduate student Eric Funabashi provided me, and that I was unable to use here. In the meantime, I will follow the work of James Farrer and the Culinary Mobilities research project at Sophia University in Tokyo, which has taken a lead in tracing the spread of Japanese food outside Japan's borders. I have a greater understanding of sushi in u.s. history, especially in California, thanks to Samuel Yamashita, who shared his massive 'sushi file' with me, read one of the chapters and whose friendship I cherish.

Another long-standing friend and colleague, Tom Lewin, graciously read the entire manuscript and offered his insights: this book and my academic life in Kansas would be much poorer without him.

Miranda Brown provided guidance to sushi in Chinese history, and I am grateful to her and Q. Edward Wang for answering my questions about ancient Chinese grains. Jordan Sand helped me track down a key image. I am grateful to Michiko Ito in the University of Kansas East Asia Library for her assistance in securing illustrations for this book and for building up the library's collection in Japanese food studies. Rick Halpern has a wonderful eye, and I am thankful to him for allowing me to include examples of his photography here. Chef Tadashi of Slurping Turtle restaurant and photographer Kara McPherson also graciously allowed me to include their photos. I am also extremely grateful to Roger Shimomura for allowing his painting on the cover and interior.

Writing about the history of sushi reminded me of the first time I tried it while in high school, and that I returned to the same restaurant a while later to succeed in convincing my father to eat a California roll despite his apprehensions. Sushi is one of the foods that makes memories, and I am glad that my work on this project has brought to mind so many meals with family and friends with whom I enjoyed 'doing sushi'.

Portions of my discussion of funazushi that appear in the beginning and the conclusion had an earlier form as 'Some Tasting Notes on Year-old Sushi: *Funazushi*, Japan's Most Ancient and Potentially Its Most Up-to-date Sushi', *Gastronomica: The Journal for Food Studies*, xx/1 (2020), pp. 34–41. I am grateful for support from the University of Kansas's Center for East Asian Studies, Office of International Programs, and Department of History, which funded a research trip to Japan in 2019 for this book. The History Department also paid for some of the illustrations and the rights to use them. During my trip, I received assistance from local food expert Greg de St Maurice and Nakagawa Tomomi, proprietor of Biwako Daughters restaurant in Shiga Prefecture. Members of the Premodern Japanese Studies (PMJS) listserve helped me resolve a 'weighty' problem concerning measurements.

This book is dedicated to my students, especially the undergraduates on my course 'The History of Sushi', which I have taught regularly at the University of Kansas and once at the University of Michigan when I was Toyota Visiting Professor in the Center for Japanese Studies. My hope is that my students think deeply about the foods that they eat and go forth to make positive changes in the world.

PHOTO ACKNOWLEDGEMENTS

The author and publishers wish to express their thanks to the below sources of illustrative material and/or permission to reproduce it. Some locations of artworks are also given below, in the interest of brevity.

Aluxum Photography/iStock.com: p. 166; The British Museum, London: p. 101; photo courtesy Chotto Matte, London/NZR Limited: p. 176; Dallas Museum of Art, TX (gift of Denni Davis Washburn and Marie Scott Miegel, 1990.240): p. 79; Freer Gallery of Art, Smithsonian Institution, Washington, DC (gift of John Fuegi and Jo Francis, F1997.37): p. 68; photos Rick Halpern, reproduced with permission: pp. 26, 27, 84, 87, 107, 109, 112, 164; Herman J. Schultheis Collection/Los Angeles Public Library: p. 141; photo Steve Hillebrand/U.S. Fish and Wildlife Service (USFWS): p. 181; photo Richard Iwaki/Unsplash: p. 53; Library of Congress, Prints and Photographs Division, Washington, DC: p. 64; photos Kara McPherson/courtesy Slurping Turtle: pp. 151, 155; The Metropolitan Museum of Art, New York: pp. 16, 46, 69; photo Chef Tadashi Nagura/courtesy Slurping Turtle: p. 13; photo Igata Naoko/ courtesy The Japan Association of Dietitian Training Institution: p. 123; courtesy Nara National Research Institute for Cultural Properties: p. 44; photo National Aeronautics and Space Administration (NASA): p. 40; National Diet Library, Tokyo: pp. 61, 95; courtesy National Museum of Ethnology, Osaka: pp. 11, 36; photo Luigi Pozzoli/Unsplash: p. 6; photos Eric C. Rath: pp. 9, 20, 48, 54, 59, 67, 82, 90, 119, 124, 179, 180, 183; Roy Andries de Groot Menu Collection, Conrad N. Hilton Library,

INDEX

Page numbers in *italics* indicate illustrations.

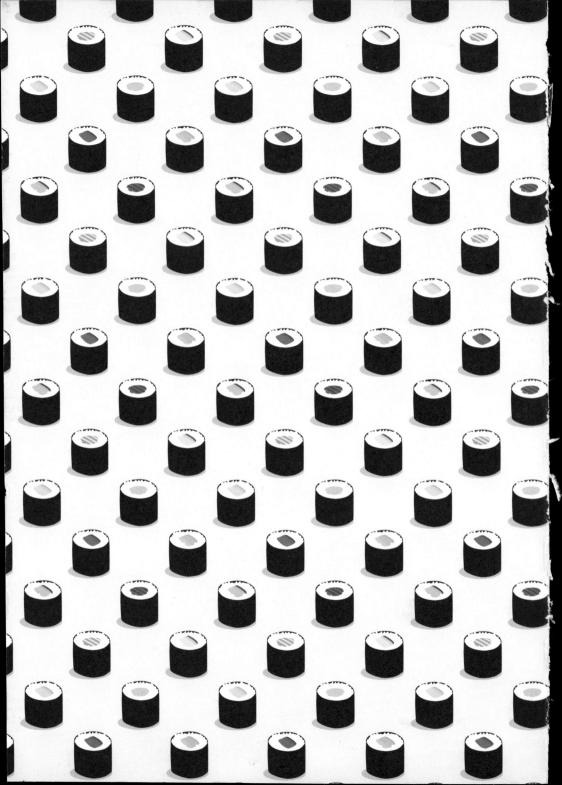